photoFREEDOM

a Big Picture approach to organizing and
scrapbooking your photographs

by Stacy Julian

Simple
Scrapbooks

Contents

Here's to you!

When I start a big project (like this book), I always go to a place near my home where there's a little bridge over a babbling brook—it sounds goofy, perhaps, but it's true. This is my happy place. I'm not really a backwoods kind of girl, but there is something extra cool about this particular spot. When I go there, I feel completely removed from the fast lane that is my life. I can clear my mind and make room for the ideas and inspiration I need. As I've thought about what I want for you and everyone who reads this book, I've decided it is clarity about scrapbooking. I want you to find liberating solutions that you can customize to your particular situation— and ultimately, I want you to find a happy place with your memories, your pictures, and your creative process.

I could dedicate this book to my family, for putting up with me when I take on more than I should, or I could dedicate this book to my colleagues at *Simple Scrapbooks* magazine for understanding my passion and believing in my vision—but what I really want to do is dedicate this book to you. You are amazing. You are clearly committed to recognizing and celebrating your life and embracing your personal "big picture." I want to help you do that in a way that will be fun and meaningful, now and in the future.

So, here's to you!

Starting points

Before we get started, you need to know that I've written this book for exactly four and a half reasons:

1. I *love* my system for organizing and storing photos, which I call my "Library of Memories."

2. I believe my system has universal application, and I know I can teach you to adapt it to your own unique needs and goals.

3. I've had lots of requests from readers of my previous book, *The Big Picture, Scrapbook Your Life and a Whole Lot More,* for information on the system that sustains my guilt-free approach to scrapbooking.

4. I really, really, *really* want to help you connect with your photographs so you can discover the magic and meaning in your memories.

4½. I tend to take on more projects than I really have time for!

As a life enthusiast, an avid photographer, and devoted scrapbooker, I'm personally acquainted with the nearly crushing anxiety that comes from trying to stay on top of the thousands of photos I take. As I have worked to celebrate the people, places, and things that are most important to me, I too have experienced that unrealistic desire to be caught up. In fact, at one point in my personal scrapbooking odyssey, my camera broke and I found myself thinking, "Phew, I'm off the hook!" That experience helped me realize that my expectations were way off, and I eventually came to grips with the fact that scrapbooking doesn't have to be an all-or-nothing hobby.

The same is true for you. It's important to realize that even if you never snap another picture for the rest of your life, you already have more photos than you can *ever* expect to showcase in your scrapbooks. Your fairy godmother could show up, wave her magic wand, and grant you several hours of uninterrupted scrapbooking time every day—and you still wouldn't have enough time to record every memory you've ever made. Now take a deep breath; I don't say this to discourage you. You don't have to banish your unfinished albums to a closet shelf and walk away—there's hope!

Somewhere between giving up entirely and pushing ahead in a mad frenzy to catch up, there is a (very) happy medium. (Hint: you're holding it in your hands right now.) This book will help you make the important decisions that lead to fantastic feelings of accomplishment and freedom, regardless of your specific goals. You'll finally be able to find and enjoy the photos you've taken; you'll be able to display them in your home and share them with those you love; and most importantly, you'll gain valuable insights into your past and present life.

In the first chapter, "My System," I'll share specifics about the organizational products I use, explaining what features to look for and why. Chapter two, "My Pictures," is all about how my photos flow from camera to creativity. And chapter three, "Your Results," will show you how other people have adapted my system to establish wonderful and inviting libraries of memories in their homes.

What is the best advice I can give you before you get started? Remember that perfection is highly overrated. (And frankly, it's just about as fun as stale bread.) All you really need is a sincere desire to become a successful (read: guilt-free) memory keeper and photographer. Let's go!

the pledge

Before you turn the page to begin this amazing process, please read, sign, and date in the presence of a witness (seriously!) the **Scrapstrong Pledge** below:

I, _____, a ready* reader who is eager to nurture my enthusiasm for scrapbooking and to be successful using and adapting Stacy's Library of Memories system, do hereby promise to uphold, to the best of my ability, the following statements:

- I will *read* this entire book (chapters one, two, *and* three) and think about Stacy's system in the context of my own life before committing time, effort, and money to implementing the ideas shared.

- Once committed, I will remain positive, open minded, and willing to change, *if* necessary.

- I will involve at least one other person in the process of adapting this system to my scrapbooking, either by allowing him or her to help me or by just asking him or her to listen and discuss ideas with me.

_____   _____
[SIGNATURE]   [DATE]

_____   _____
[WITNESS SIGNATURE]   [DATE]

It's time to take charge and make this hobby a guilt-free and sustainable part of your life! You can do this!

*Please see facing page.

Note: Scrapstrong bracelets are sold through *Scrapbook.com*, and 100 percent of the proceeds are donated to foundations such as Lance Armstrong's Livestrong foundation and the Huntsman Cancer Foundation.

I'm going to be perfectly honest with you . . .

You may not be ready for this book. The Library of Memories system and the ideas I'm about to share were born out of my own need for another way to scrapbook, but I'm fully aware that everyone's situation is different. You may not have a backlog of photos or feel the pressure to scrapbook every memory you have. Your scrapbook story may include fewer people than mine. (Children and large extended families generally mean more pictures and more pressure!) You may have just started scrapbooking and be blissfully unaware of the overwhelming expectations I have felt.

If that's the case, then good for you. You're probably not interested in investing time and effort in a new scrapbooking system and approach. And you know what? That's 100 percent okay!

But if you choose to keep reading, remember that the all-or-nothing rule doesn't apply to this book or my system. You might be ready to embrace it all—or maybe you'll only find relevance in parts and pieces of what I share. Either way, I'm thrilled you are scrapbooking and I'm anxious to be a resource to you. I'm also eager to grant you permission (if you need it) to let go, be more authentic, and have more fun.

Ready or not, here we go!

Meet little Stacy!

Throughout this book, there will be sidebars full of little nuggets that I really want you to take to heart. If you see a little Stacy, it means stop, drop, and read. Trust me. This is good stuff!

Words of advice

Take it from other scrapbookers who have already implemented the Library of Memories system:

"Trust Stacy. The system really works! And don't get so hung up on small details (the color or type of your albums, for example) that you completely miss out on the concepts and structure behind the Library of Memories system."

MARTY OSTERHAUDT, MANLIUS, NY

"Take it slow. Do things week by week, in baby steps. This is not a weekend project!"

BROOKE SCHUMACHER, DHAHRAN, SAUDI ARABIA

"Don't feel pressured to buy the products that Stacy recommends, especially in the beginning. Use what you have until you have a better idea of how the system will work for you."

MICHELLE SICOTTE, WHITEHORSE, YUKON, CANADA

"Don't sweat it if you can't find the exact album or if they discontinue something you were using. Your family changes and grows, and so should your Library of Memories system."

GAYE LARSEN, SAN DIEGO, CA

"Don't pull everything out at once! Set a timer for 15 minutes and only get out what you might accomplish in that time—then take a break. This will keep you from getting overwhelmed by a new process."

JULIE CORRIGAN, HOLLISTER, CA

"Definitely reorganize your old layouts into your own library. For me it had the greatest impact in helping me understand where I have been with my scrapbooking and where I want to go."

MAUREEN SARGENT, DEDHAM, MA

"Get the Storage Albums and Category Drawers right away! They are the heart of the Library of Memories system and will make your life much easier."

TAMMY THOMAS, OAK CITY, UT

"Go through the process as outlined, start to finish. It's the only way you can really catch the vision of the whole system. Fiddle with it later, adapt it if you want, but the process is really an important thing to experience. Only after I caught the big picture could I see how everything worked together."

CATHERINE ALLAN, AMERICAN FALLS, ID

"Have a trash can nearby— two, if possible."

MOLLY MCCARTHY, OAK PARK, CA

"Work through the system, try everything, and then make it your own. The Library of Memories system is meant to be personalized. Don't worry about how everything fits together, just know that it does."

LAURIE WEAVER, HOUSTON, TX

"Approach the system with an open mind and be willing to learn. It will change the way you scrapbook your memories. It is so worth the effort to become a guilt-free scrapbooker."

LINDA MILLS, SURREY, BC, CANADA

chapter

1

My system

Scrapbooking is a great and purposeful hobby, but it can definitely turn from fun to frustrating if you don't feel organized. When you have a master plan for sorting, storing, and tracking all of the photos, memorabilia, and stories that are meaningful to you, you can keep your energy focused on preserving memories. You'll be able to respond to creative inspiration with enthusiasm (this means assembling a layout!) instead of wasting that energy on the hunt for a particular photo. That's why I'm so anxious to share with you the details of my Library of Memories system.

In this chapter...

- You'll learn about the three essential components of my Library of Memories system, the foundation of my guilt-free approach.

- You'll be able to pick and choose from nine additional components (I call them "extras") in order to customize my system to your lifestyle.

- You'll realize that having a personal plan is critical, and that it can and should evolve over time.

chapter 1: preview

If I say "I scrapbooked last night," what visual image

pops into your head? I bet you're picturing me in the act of assembling a layout, right? You probably see me with a sheet or two of cardstock and a stack photos in front of me, with my paper trimmer and lots of fun, colorful accents nearby. If so, you could be buying into a common misconception about this hobby of ours—one that I need to address before we can move on.

You see, the term *scrapbooking* does not just refer to the assembly of pages. Scrapbooking actually describes an ongoing, multi-dimensional spectrum of activities that begins with an awareness of your life, followed by a desire to photograph and record your day-to-day experiences, ultimately resulting in scrapbook albums that are overflowing with colorful, perspective-laden layouts, each of which contributes in some small way to the story of your life and heritage. (Whew, that was a mouthful!)

When you stop to think about all the preparation and effort that goes into even one scrapbook page, it's no wonder so many of us have worn thin the excuse, "I don't have time." While I'd be first in line to add more hours to my day, it truly isn't more time that I need. What we all need to do is step back and (here I go again) take a big-picture look at the variety of activities that make up scrapbooking. Then we can discover doable ways of incorporating these activities into our daily lives—in small chunks.

Think about it this way: when you're ordering prints online, you're scrapbooking. When you stop to write down something your child says or tuck a receipt or wrapper into that special pocket in your wallet, you're scrapbooking. When you stop and sketch something in the grocery store or start a collection of paint swatches or call Grandma for her secret to smooth gravy, you're placing value on the things that make up a great scrapbook. The challenge comes in tracking, organizing, and prioritizing all of these tidbits so they're accessible to you when inspiration for a layout strikes. And this is where my Library of Memories system comes in!

In order to help you understand how my system functions, I've divided its elements into two categories: the *essentials* and the *extras*. The *essentials* are made up of three need-to-get tools that are fundamental to the success of this approach. The nine *extras* are nice-to-have items that may or may not apply to you now or in the future.

In the pages that follow, I'll show you exactly which products comprise my system and advise you on what to look for when you purchase your own.

Colorful
You.

ESSENTIAL NO. 1

Storage Binders

My **Storage Binders** are a must-have because they help me temporarily store several years' worth of printed snapshots in chronological order. They allow me to quickly peruse, pull, and use prints for various scrapbooking projects (a much better option than digging through photo sleeves and digital files). In these basic, no-frills binders, my prints are protected from fingerprints, and they stay in order until I'm ready to remove them.

WHAT I USE

I use navy blue leather Pioneer Storage Binders (available online at *scrapbook.com*) that are designed to showcase three 4 x 6 photos on each page. (These are also referred to as three-up albums.) To get the most out of my binders, I use a DYMO label maker to tag the spines with removable labels, and I replace the labels when I change the contents of my binders.

WHAT TO LOOK FOR

- Archival photo albums with three-ring bindings that will allow you to easily add and remove individual pages

- Archival-quality photo sleeves with sturdy seams that will hold more than one print per pocket (I often stack similar prints in the same pocket—more on this on page 48)

sound familiar?

"I had all my scrapped photos in one place and all my unscrapped photos in another, chronologically, by year. I had to thumb through the actual year's worth of photos to find the one I was looking for, and if I couldn't remember what year it was taken, I was in real trouble."

CATHERINE ALLAN, TWIN FALLS, ID

ESSENTIAL NO. 2

Category Drawers or file boxes

My **Category Drawers** serve as long-term storage for a relatively small selection of my photo prints. Each drawer is labeled with one of the four main categories I use to classify all of my layouts—People We Love, Places We Go, Things We Do, and All About Us— (I will explain more about these categories on page 62). These drawers help me quickly find photos of specific people, places, and things—a huge timesaver when I sit down to make a layout.

WHAT I USE

I use metal index-card cabinets (available by special order from large office supply chain stores) that hold lots of loose, individual prints and allow easy access and retrieval. Note: As a companion piece to drawers or boxes, I also use acid-free tabbed divider cards to mark subcategories within each drawer or box.

WHAT TO LOOK FOR

- Accessibility (I recommend drawer-style storage that you can access without even removing a lid)

- An adjustable mechanism that will keep photos upright (you will need to be able to easily adjust the capacity of each category drawer over time)

- Durability (this is an active storage system that you will use every single day)

- Large capacity (they will serve their purpose better if you have one drawer or box for each category)

a note

I've said it before, but it bears repeating. **You can only scrapbook in the way you are organized.** If you yearn to embrace your inner journalist, make connections that only you can make, and share truly interesting and insightful stories, then you've got to store your photos so they can help you! Category Drawers are the secret weapon that make it possible for me to be an authentic and intentional scrapbooker. Ignore that voice in your head that says "take my pictures out of order, is she crazy?" Instead, listen to me; the sooner you set up Category Drawers and begin filling them up, the sooner you'll be able to celebrate the stuff that really matters. Do you think I'd really write a book and lie to you?

trust me

Trust me, the essentials are essential. I've been asked why I maintain both Storage Binders and Category Drawers. The answer lies in what I have just shared. Together, these two storage tools help me corral, view, prioritize, and scrapbook my pictures—as well as recognize connections between individual prints. I can create pages and projects that speak to the length and the breadth of my story. This is a very satisfying and inspiring thing!

ESSENTIAL NO. 3

Library Albums

My **Library Albums** are the final resting place for my
completed layouts. They make my pages easily accessible
for family and friends, and they're the automatic home
for my scrapbooking creations. I started with four albums—
one each for People We Love, Places We Go, Things We Do, and
All About Us—but I've added more albums over time.

WHAT I USE

I use D-ring Modern albums from American Crafts in four
colors (green, red, brown, and pink), each representing one of
my main categories. Since I create 8½ x 11 and 12 x 12 pages, I
have albums in both sizes for each category. And as my library
of layouts grows, I continue to add more of the same albums
to my system. To label my Library Albums, I use circle tags
covered with cardstock that matches the album cover.

WHAT TO LOOK FOR

- Three-ring binding (to make it easy to add new layouts so
  your friends and family can enjoy your efforts immediately)

- Albums that accommodate standard page protectors
  (these make the ongoing task of storing pages simple
  and affordable)

- Style and materials that appeal to you (think about where
  in your home you'll store or display your albums: the colors,
  style, and materials should complement their surroundings)

- Future availability of the albums (if uniformity is important
  to you)

trust me

You get what you pay for when it comes to these fundamental
components of the Library of Memories system. I'm not saying you
need to go overboard, but please purchase the highest quality
essentials you can afford. You'll thank me down the road!

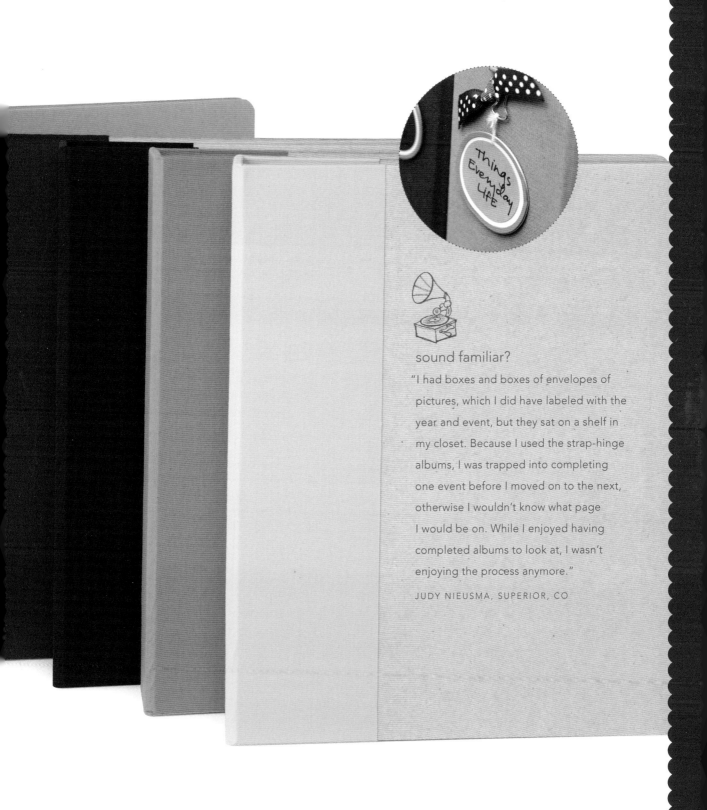

sound familiar?

"I had boxes and boxes of envelopes of pictures, which I did have labeled with the year and event, but they sat on a shelf in my closet. Because I used the strap-hinge albums, I was trapped into completing one event before I moved on to the next, otherwise I wouldn't know what page I would be on. While I enjoyed having completed albums to look at, I wasn't enjoying the process anymore."

JUDY NIEUSMA, SUPERIOR, CO

EXTRA NO. 1

Memorabilia notebook or file

My memorabilia notebook serves as safe, temporary storage for certificates, letters, newspaper articles, brochures, and other noteworthy documents I want to include in my scrapbooks. This simple notebook is a short-term holding place where these items can stay organized and accessible until I find or take pictures to accompany them.

WHAT I USE

I use the Creative Page Planner/Work Binder from Memory Dock. This oversized binder, with its multi-pocket planner sheets, accommodates the large and small memorabilia that I'm saving for future use on scrapbook pages.

WHAT TO LOOK FOR

- Distinct folders or protectors that keep individual pieces of memorabilia separate until related pictures can be found and stored together

- Portability (so you can keep it with you while you're browsing through a Storage Binder or looking through a Category Drawer)

a note

My memorabilia binder is not designed to store *all* of my memorabilia, just the pieces I know I want to scrapbook. (See pages 32 and 72 for more information about storing and using memorabilia.)

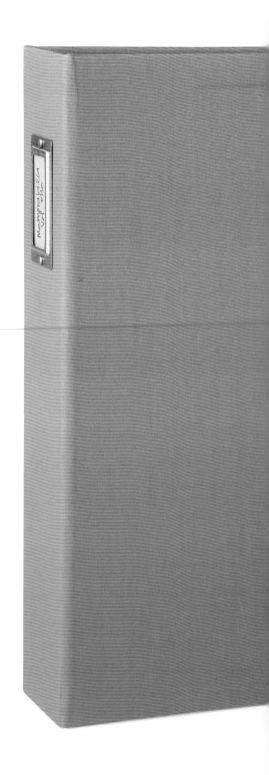

reality check

Do I file all my potentially "scrapworthy" memorabilia right away? Heavens no. I've got a small wire basket where I collect stuff until I have time to review it and place it in either the notebook or the trash.

EXTRA NO. 2

Photo organization software

My photo-organizing program allows me to tag and group the digital images that are stored on my computer and external hard drive. I love it because it lets me quickly sift through photos and locate the best and most scrappable pictures—an extremely helpful feature when it comes to deciding which pictures to print.

WHAT I USE

I use iPhoto (from the iLife software package) for Macintosh computers. When I had a PC, I used the Adobe Photoshop Album program, which is now available with Photoshop 4.0.

WHAT TO LOOK FOR

- Ability to comprehensively view every image on your computer in the order they were taken

- A tag or copy feature that enables you to set up folders where copies of selected digital images can be grouped and viewed together

- Basic editing tools that allow cropping, color adjustments, and quick-fix options

a note

Visit *simplescrapbooksmag.com/software* to learn more about the variety of photo organization software options available to you.

personal opinion

I repeat: you can only scrapbook in the way you are organized. If your pictures are not organized at all, you will be continually frustrated. If you can't easily browse through your pictures when you feel inspired to use them, you will quickly become discouraged. If your photos are stored or grouped only in chronological order, you'll be limited in the topics you can scrapbook. That doesn't sound like much fun to me!

EXTRA NO. 3

Materials files, folders, or containers

My materials folders provide a temporary home for the supplies I'm using for ongoing projects. I store cardstock, embellishments, scraps, photos, and more in individual pockets within my file folder—so when I have some free time to work on the project, everything I need is right at my fingertips.

WHAT I USE

I use a dozen or more large nesting folders from Croppin' Companion. I like them because they're transparent, and I can easily view their contents without opening them. They also fit vertically on my shelf, which saves a lot of space.

WHAT TO LOOK FOR

- Translucency

- Expandable pockets to provide space for a changing number of projects

- Durability for long-term use (at crops and at home)

trust me

Materials files are worth considering. I feel like I talk and write about them often (for good reason!), but stick with me here, even if you think you've heard this before. Once you've decided to create a theme album or other project one of the smartest (most efficient) things you can do is gather and store together the photos and consumable products you plan to use as you update it.

GIRLS' WEEKEND

a note

Every year, I have a girls' weekend. And every year, I add a few more pages to the album. And every year, can you guess what makes this process fun and painless? Everything I need to work on it is tucked into a materials file and ready to go!

2003 Questions

One. Is your life at this point what y
when you were a little girl?

Two. What have you done that wou
your friends in high School?

Three. Blank has been more diffic
be.

Four. Blank has been easier than

Five. What are you doing or acc
now that surprises you?

Six. If time and money wasn't a
you pursue?

Seven. Blank always makes me

List five personal highlights fo
respond to the five relationshi

= 2003 =

ite of offices for a group of
ew home; Chanda getting
son (and preparing a room
ld with the Julians

s many, but limiting it to
e the heart to heart
wd at the Magic

would most like to
ss to work hard for

ry because she is so

sted in others. She
favorite
IS variety.
nd her "true
oming a nurse.

EXTRA NO. 4

School of Life file box

With four children in school and a growing collection of school-related memorabilia to keep track of, I absolutely need a drop-and-go file for each kid. My big Rubbermaid file box includes a folder for every grade from kindergarten through twelfth grade for each child.

They allow me to save (and sift through) schoolwork, report cards, certificates, and awards before they have a chance to pile up and get lost. I set up all of my folders at once (years ago) so I would be ready to gather school-related memorabilia from now through the graduation of my youngest.

a note

I have another set of albums, outside of the four main topics in my Library of Memories system, that I call "School of Life" albums. Using the items I'm gathering into these file boxes, I'm creating 12 x 12 scrapbooks for each of my children (featuring chronological highlights from their academic lives) that they can take with them when they leave the nest. You can learn more about the concept and format of these albums in my previous books, *Simple Scrapbooks* and *The Big Picture*.

WHAT I USE

I use a big Rubbermaid file tote (how's that for simple?), with an easy-to-remove lid. Inside, I have hanging file folders labeled by child and grade.

WHAT TO LOOK FOR

• Large size (to fit school portraits and sports team photos)

• Capacity to hold hanging files

personal opinion

The layouts I create and store in my Library Albums are for me. (Read: I do not create duplicate layouts for my children to eventually take with them. Read again: the All About Clark album that is part of our Library of Memories stays with me—it's mine!) However, I feel the evidence of my kids' growth, achievements, and accomplishments belongs to them. And these School of Life albums take care of the obligation I feel to create scrapbooks my kids can take with them.

system

EXTRA NO. 5

Family tree drawers or files

Because I have a growing collection of heritage photos and important documents related to my family's history, I needed a place to safely store and organize them. My family tree drawers provide easy access (no lids to remove or endless stacking and restacking required), plus protection from dust and sunlight. I have one drawer for my husband and me, and one drawer for each of our parents and grandparents.

WHAT I USE

I use shallow 8½ x 14 drawers from We R Memory Keepers (part of the Memory Dock system), and I label the front with a simple white tab.

WHAT TO LOOK FOR

- Limited exposure to light

- Protection from dust

- Capacity to hold large photos

personal opinion

Collect as much information from older family members as you can, even if you're not ready to "scrapbook" it yet. Send out a short questionnaire to grandparents—ask them to use their handwriting if possible and to sign their name at the bottom. So easy and absolutely priceless.

a note

I love this drawer system so much that I also have a drawer designated for professional portraits of our immediate family and drawers labeled "people," "places," and "things," where I store the occasional 5 x 7 or 8 x 10 prints I order. (See page 59 for more on enlargements.)

EXTRA NO. 6

Cultural memorabilia box

I'm sure it's obvious by now, but I love saving the everyday snippets of life that I often refer to as "ephemera of the future"—things like product labels, receipts, and tags. To help me incorporate these daily tidbits into my scrapbooks, I store them in a little container that I can easily dig through when I'm making pages and projects.

WHAT I USE

I use a small, lightweight box with a hinged lid and clasp—something I actually found at a discount store for less than $5.

WHAT TO LOOK FOR

• Small, lightweight containers

• Cute and easy to access

trust me

Cute helps. What I mean is, anytime you can store things in an attractive box vs. a not-so-attractive box, go for attractive. When you retrieve something from a cute container, you feel cute, and when you feel cute—well, that's a good thing!

what about … storage?

There are so many options when it comes to storage containers, but how do you decide what's right for you? Just when you make up your mind, you'll inevitably see what someone else is using and question your choice. Having a personalized plan and an understanding of your creative process is key. I recommend using the expert information and solution-packed workbook in *The Organized & Inspired Scrapbooker* by Wendy Smedley and Aby Garvey.

EXTRA NO. 7

Family words file and small notebooks

I'm convinced that actual words spoken are far more telling than any caption I could write. For years I have used a collection of small notebooks scattered around my home to record sound bites from my everyday life. I love that these quotes eventually make it to my family words file, which sits in my studio ready to inspire me. Every so often, I gather up these notebooks, tear out individual pages, and place them in my family words file, behind the quoted person's tab.

WHAT I USE

I use a variety of little notebooks and a standard-sized recipe box for filing my notes. The notebooks I use most are in my car's glove compartment, my purse, and a kitchen drawer. I try to keep one in each bedroom, too.

WHAT TO LOOK FOR

• Small, portable notebooks (lots of them!)

• A tabbed container to sort your notes into

You can't make this stuff up!

My collection of writer's notebooks helps me "get the story." These strategically placed notebooks are the paper equivalent of carrying my camera around—so I'm always able and ready to capture a memorable quote. I generally jot down the name of the person I'm quoting, the date, and the circumstances that elicited the memorable comments.

"Whenever I eat Grandma's jam I think of her—not of Grandpa or anyone else, just Grandma. I really love her jam."
Trey, while eating breakfast, February 9, 2007

"If a kid says they did their homework, parents should just believe them and not ask too many questions."
Chase, in response to a dinner-table question

"There are four jobs for me when I grow up: zookeeper, ice cream seller, decorator, and cleaner-upper. Yep, four jobs I'm good at."
Taft, while helping me clean and set up for a party in February 2007

"If I got that for my birthday, I'd be crying right now."
Trey, after Clark opened his new T1-84 silver edition graphing calculator on his 14th birthday

Clark's response: **"You're joking, right?"**

"I'm sure third grade will be cool, but college is the best. They have a library that is outside the building and it's huge. And there are dorms—so you don't even have to come home!"
Trey, on the way to back-to-school night, September 5, 2007

"I did a parotidectomy all by myself on an 80-year-old woman, then an endoscopic sinus surgery, two sets of tubes, a tonsil, and saw 17 patients—plus made phone calls, dictated notes, and didn't eat breakfast or lunch. I feel sick!"
Geof, after a long day at work, February 26, 2007

reality check

Please don't make this notebook thing hard! Your notebooks don't need to match or be assigned to particular people or topics. The important thing is to have them close by when you need them, so you can write down the words while they're fresh.

EXTRA NO. 8

Cold storage photo boxes

When it comes time to clean out my Storage Binders and remove photos that have remained unscrapbooked for years (read more about this on page 70), I have a choice: throw them away, or move into long-term storage. Yes, I throw some away (and it's so freeing!). Other photos I file away in photo boxes. This helps me keep older photos safely organized in a back room while allowing me to focus my scrapbooking on the newer photos in my Storage Binders and Category Drawers.

WHAT I USE

Archival-quality photo boxes from *Exposures.com* with removable lids. I customized mine with patterned paper and rub-ons.

WHAT TO LOOK FOR

- Stackability so they're easy to tuck away on a shelf

- Capacity to hold hundreds of photos

personal opinion

Far too many of us are frustrated by the feeling that we are wasting precious creative time by not using it effectively (and no, 45 minutes spent searching out a particular photo is not an effective use of time). One of the best ways to save time is to limit the number of photos we have to sort through. We must learn to discipline ourselves in a few critical areas of preparation so we can experience more creative productivity later.

Square-punch picture drawers

As I was revisiting old pictures that I had placed in Cold Storage, I decided to pull out my square punch and start punching out the faces of my children and others. (Sound weird? Stick with me!) Within a few minutes, I knew I was on to something—I knew I would enjoy having a collection of thumbnail-type images always at my fingertips. This newest addition to my Library of Memories lineup is a fun way to get mileage out of unused photos, and it's a great place to fish for cropped pictures of people I love.

WHAT I USE

I use six little plastic drawers that I had previously purchased to store small embellishments. (No hang-ups here about recycling storage containers!) I labeled one for each child and one for both Geoff and me.

IMPORTANT FEATURES

- One-handed access for easy drop-and-go storage
- Stackability to save space at your workstation

my
system

chapter 1: review

Now that I've introduced you to my Library of Memories system, let's review the basic philosophy behind it.

My secret to creative freedom is found in my two-fold approach to photo storage (Storage Binders and Category Drawers) and the fact that there is no sequential expectation placed on me by my album system. Because I don't have a 2005, 2006, or 2007 album, I also don't have the pressure to fill them up. I don't feel an obligation to the calendar. I can flip through my Storage Binders to easily locate event-based pictures, or I can turn to my Category Drawers to find pictures that illustrate personality, relationships, and human connection. I no longer feel behind in October if I haven't scrapbooked Halloween from the previous year. In fact, I actually feel encouraged to let pictures of annual events sit in my Storage Binders for a few years, because then I have more creative options!

My Storage Binders hold the bulk of my current pictures, and as I look through them, I'm continually reminded of the happenings in our home. Since I have five years of photos temporarily stored in these binders, and limited time to scrapbook, my Storage Binders help me subconsciously prioritize which events, celebrations, and milestones to showcase on pages—and which I will skip over or highlight in a theme album or other project. For example, if

I have two dozen pictures from a camping trip that I have not felt inspired to scrapbook for three years, I might decide to pull a handful of the best pictures, re-file (or triage) them into my Category Drawers, and then move the remaining photos into Cold Storage. Condensing the contents of my Storage Binders this way gives me a huge sense of relief because it allows me to recognize and focus on the events that are most relevant to our story.

My Category Drawers provide a place for a few event-based pictures to mingle with more random, everyday photos and emerge as evidence of larger patterns or connections. Five years after moving those camping pictures, maybe I'll be looking through the photos behind the Summer tab in my Things drawer and discover a picture of 4-year-old Clark eating a s'more around the campfire and a photo of him as a teenager helping his little brother roast a marshmallow at Grandma's lake house. Seeing two pictures like that side by side would make it easy to see change, growth, and the influence of seasonal rituals on family relationships. That's what I call an "Aha, I get it!" moment.

And here's the really exciting part: I get to decide how to scrapbook this connection and where to put it in my Library of Memories!

chapter

2

My photos

I've already introduced you to the three essential and nine extra elements I use to manage my pictures, words, and memorabilia. Now let's delve more deeply into how these parts become a connected and functioning whole. In the pages that follow, I'll show you how I actually use each piece in the context of my scrapbooking studio and my life.

In this chapter...

- You'll learn about the process my photos travel through to get from camera to layout.

- You'll discover how the essentials and extras I told you about in chapter 1 can work together to make scrapbooking more fun and inspiring.

- You'll find dozens of practical tips to help you spend your time scrapbooking the memories that are most important to you and your family.

chapter 2: preview

My sister Darci used to be a school teacher. I remember visiting her first-grade classroom the day before school started one year. Everything was set up and ready to go—the desks, chairs, books, and reading corner. All were immaculate. She showed me around, full of enthusiasm, chatting about the curriculum and the fun ideas she had planned. Then she turned and said half-jokingly, "If only the children didn't have to come and mess it all up!"

That's kind of how I feel about my scrapbooking sometimes—*my system would work so well without all the pictures to complicate things!* But obviously, the pictures are pretty essential to this hobby—so it's important for me to use a system that keeps them accessible in an inspiring way. Just like Darci's perfectly prepared classroom was useless without students, the well-planned components of my Library of Memories system aren't much good without the photos flowing through them.

My system is more than just the physical Storage Binders, Category Drawers, and Library Albums. It's a series of processes I follow on a regular basis to keep my pictures flowing through the various elements you learned about in chapter 1. The very reason my system works for me, *and* the reason it will work for you, is the fact that it's not linear (step one followed by step two, etc.). I can pick up almost anywhere I want for 15 minutes or 3 hours, work on something, and know that my time

was well spent. I have to maintain each part or process, but I don't have to maintain them in a specific order for a specific amount of time. It's all very flexible.

In the pages that follow, I'll show you exactly how my photos flow from my camera to my computer to my Storage Binders to my Category Drawers and, finally, to layouts in my Library Albums. Plus, I'll give you some advice on how to adapt these processes for your photos.

a note

I suggest you read through this section once and then pull out the poster from the back of the book. See if you can: 1) Follow the sketch like you would a map when traveling from a starting point to a final destination, and 2) Share this sketch with someone else and explain the purpose of each element and the role it plays in the overall Library of Memories plan. (Why do this? Because often the best way to learn something is to teach it to someone else.) Refer back to the text as needed and begin to envision your own sketch or map. What will it look like and how might it differ from mine?

CELEBRATE
WHO YOU ARE

do the math!

This chapter is all about my pictures, but first let's talk about your pictures for just a second. Before reading on, stop right here and guesstimate how many unscrapped pictures you have (both prints and digital images) at this very moment.

How many pictures in each of these categories do you think you have?

- [ ] ⋯⋯Undeveloped film

- [ ] ⋯⋯Snapshots stored in photo envelopes

- [ ] ⋯⋯Photos in magnetic albums

- [ ] ⋯⋯Unframed school and family portraits
(the JC Penney or Kiddie Candids kind)

- [ ] ⋯⋯Pictures from your (or anyone else's) childhood

- [ ] ⋯⋯Heritage or one-of-a-kind photos

- [ ] ⋯⋯Images on your computer that you have not yet printed

- [ ] ⋯⋯**Write your grand total here.**

reality check

Here are five "photo truths" that help me move past common hurdles:

- Not all pictures are created equal.

- It's really hard to be inspired by pictures I can't see and touch and hold.

- Leftovers happen—and it's OK not to use all the photos I initially selected for a page.

- It's OK to throw a picture away. (It is!)

- Most pictures don't need to be labeled with names and a date.

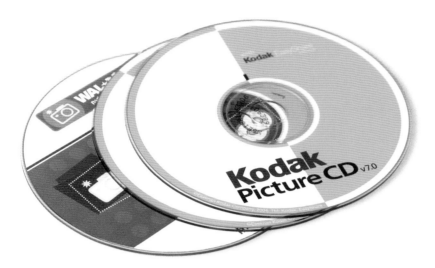

With that total in mind, review the following statements and check off either agree or disagree:

I have more pictures than I can scrapbook in my lifetime.

☐ AGREE   ☐ DISAGREE

I take two or three times more photos with my digital camera than I ever did with film!

☐ AGREE   ☐ DISAGREE

I often feel an obligation to enhance, tweak, or alter my digital images before printing them.

☐ AGREE   ☐ DISAGREE

I haven't ordered prints because I might want to custom print an image in a different size for a specific page or project.

☐ AGREE   ☐ DISAGREE

Since becoming a "scrapbooker," I have felt guilt for pictures that are in magnetic albums. I also feel it is somehow unacceptable to display pictures in standard photo albums.

☐ AGREE   ☐ DISAGREE

I worry that if I create a layout about an event, I might find or be given additional pictures of that event later on and then be frustrated.

☐ AGREE   ☐ DISAGREE

In some cases, where I have hundreds of photos that belong together (for vacations, holidays, etc.), I've wondered if it's OK to use some in a theme album and some on pages, saving others for future projects. I worry that pictures that were taken together need to end up together.

☐ AGREE   ☐ DISAGREE

I expect myself to create duplicate or at least very similar pages about events that involve several members of my family (i.e., one for each person's album).

☐ AGREE   ☐ DISAGREE

I find myself thinking, "If scrapbooking is supposed to be so much fun, why do I feel overwhelmed, confused, and frustrated by it?"

☐ AGREE   ☐ DISAGREE

Even when I do enjoy a windfall of FREE time for scrapbooking, I have no idea where to start.

☐ AGREE   ☐ DISAGREE

how'd you do?

45

Gathering and sorting a lifetime of prints

Based on the questions you just answered, I'm going to assume that you have years and years of unorganized pictures. Don't worry, you're not alone. Take a deep breath and say out loud, "there's no time like the present," and then dig in, following these six steps:

1 **Find and gather to one place (preferably a low-traffic area in your home with a table) all your boxes, bins, bags, and envelopes of pictures.** (Don't forget the loose ones you just tossed into that drawer by the phone.) And, yes, grab those fourteen magnetic albums, too. Don't get overwhelmed. You need to have all of your pictures in front of you for this—and you'll be glad you did.

DATE COMPLETED {_____}

2 **Group the boxes, bins, bags, envelopes, and magnetic albums by decade.** In other words, do NOT deal with individual prints yet—just stick with the containers they are in.

DATE COMPLETED {_____}

3 **Create a quick timeline table (see Resources on page 124) with years running down the side and names of people you scrapbook for running across the top.** Make a note *in pencil* of major events like marriages, births, moves, new jobs, school advancements, etc. Use this timeline as a reference as you sort your pictures so you don't have to do mental acrobatics each time you're puzzled by when a picture was taken. ("Let's see, when did we go to Hawaii? It was before McKenzie was born, but after John and Lisa's wedding." Voila! You know where those pictures go.)

DATE COMPLETED {_____}

We're not done yet! Flip the page for steps 4 – 7.

trust me

You *will* be able to move past the paradigm that pictures should always remain in date order. Just keep in mind that what you crave is order, not necessarily chronological order. The creative freedoms you'll enjoy at the end of this process will more than make up for the time and energy you're investing now. Hang in there!

④ **Begin with one decade of pictures and sort them into piles by year.** Again, don't remove individual prints unless you need to. Start by simply moving the boxes, envelopes, and albums into smaller groups by year. Only sort individual prints as needed, referring to your timeline for help with chronology.

DATE COMPLETED {____}

Are you still with me? Keep going! You can do it!

⑤ **Now focus on a year's worth of photos at a time, and start sorting individual prints into four piles**—one for each season or quarter. Don't worry too much about precision here, and keep a trash can nearby so you can easily toss photos you no longer need to keep.

DATE COMPLETED {____}

⑥ **Begin slipping photos into your Storage Binders.** (Feel free to place multiple photos in a photo pocket, like I do.) Set aside photos that you don't really want to scrapbook, but you also don't want to toss; you'll save them in your Cold Storage photo boxes for future access. Don't panic when you come across additional pictures that belong in a Storage Binder you have already "filled." Simply add some additional pocket pages to the binder and slip them in.

DATE COMPLETED {____}

This may seem like a lengthy process, but I promise that it's worth your time. The time you spend on these seven steps will save you countless hours down the road.

what about … chronology?

When I was little my mother had a Kodak 110 camera. When we celebrated a holiday, she would line everybody up and snap a single photo. Every 3 months or so, she would take the film in to be developed. The 12 (yes, 12) pictures she got back depicted a range of events and activities. It made perfect sense to compile these pictures in an album in chronological order, providing a chance for us to look back and review the highlights.

Fast forward 30 years, and think about how different your photographic approach is from your mother's. I bet you take dozens of pictures on every holiday, birthday, and major event, not to mention all the photos you take in-between. As scrapbookers, most of us now use our digital cameras to capture the subtleties of mood, emotion, personality, and relationships—not just to chronicle annual events. Photography today is as much about inspiration as it is about documentation. So if you want scrapbooks that truly showcase the colorful point of view you are freezing through your lens, chronology is an outdated approach. I truly believe in this. Expecting yourself to keep up with annual albums not only leaves you feeling perpetually behind, it also limits your creative potential as a storyteller and artist.

what about … negatives?

There are many options for organizing and tracking print negatives, and I must admit I've attempted (quite unsuccessfully) to employ most of them. I used to spend hours carefully categorizing and labeling negatives, just in case I needed to make reprints one day. When I realized I had only ordered reprints from negatives two or three times *ever*, I let go of the self-imposed pressure to track them. Now I'm perfectly content as long as my negatives are safe—organized or not. I simply toss them (already encased in their protective sleeves) into a large envelope or photo box and store them at my husband's office. I figure that if, heaven forbid, my printed pictures were lost in a disaster, I wouldn't mind digging through unlabeled negatives.

personal opinion

Labeling and storing negatives can be extremely time-consuming; please don't let this task keep you from scrapbooking. The most important thing you can do with your negatives is to gather them up and find a place outside of your home to store them. If you don't have time to organize negatives now, don't do it. Focus instead on scrapbooking your memories!

reality check

It's not a big deal if a photo taken in April ends up in a summer pile. It's also not critical that all photos are displayed in exact sequential order inside a Storage Binder. Remember, these binders are an active, temporary form of storage designed to help pictures flow through your system, eventually finding their way onto scrapbook pages! It takes only a few minutes to view the contents of an entire Storage Binder, so excessive attention to order is not the best use of your time at this early point in the process.

Gathering, sorting, and storing snapshots taken before 1980

Generally speaking, the further back we go, the fewer snapshots we have to deal with. But that doesn't mean old photos should be forgotten. I recommend sorting pre-1980 snapshots first by decade and then year and season, if needed. You may be able to store 5, 10, or even 15 years' worth of pictures in one Storage Binder, especially if you slip similar photos into the same pocket. If you feel the need to create a backup of these often one-of-a-kind prints, put them into a Storage Binder first and then remove them a few at a time for scanning and saving to a disk.

what about ... heritage photos?

I have a relatively small collection of photos and memorabilia from my parents and grandparents on both sides of my family. I sort and store such photos, letters, documents, and other information in archival drawers (see page 30) by person. For now, this approach allows me both drop-and-go storage and easy retrieval. Please know that I am not yet comfortable calling myself a family historian. Documenting and preserving a large collection of very old photos in a variety of sizes is far beyond the scope of what I'm discussing in this book. I recommend a comprehensive read of Becky Higgins' book, *Family History Scrapbooking* (published by Primedia, 2006), if you are interested in researching, archiving, and compiling historical stories and albums.

CASE STUDY

Rescued baby album

I recently rescued my childhood photos from a yellowed and deteriorating baby book compiled by my mother during my growing-up years. I simply tagged the spine of an empty Storage Binder with the labels "Stacy's Childhood" and "1965–1980," and slipped in photos as I removed them from the original book. One of my goals for the project was basic preservation, since the book's contents were beginning to discolor and fade. As I removed photos, I also copied or cut out information my mother had recorded in her handwriting. With little effort, I preserved the original photos and words in a safe, accessible place—until I decide how I want to use them all.

Our Baby

I want to use and enjoy my pictures, not get hung up on
archiving them. For that reason I often scrapbook original
photos without making copies of them. Sure, I avoid doing
irreversible things to them, like cropping, distressing, and
painting, etc.—but I definitely love to use them!

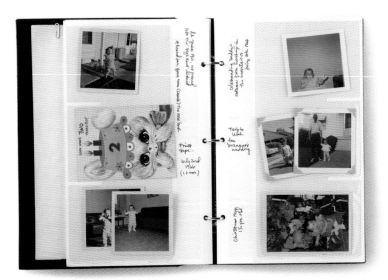

STORAGE BINDER

MATERIALS FILE FOR MY HAPPY
CHILDHOOD ALBUM

As I focused on preservation, I came up with an idea for a doable project that would allow me to capture the essence of my childhood while preserving the look and feel of my original baby book. I started with a pink 9 x 9 album that reminded me of my original baby book, then I gathered cardstock, patterned paper, and embellishments into a Materials File. I chose a handful of the prints I remember best (from the Storage Binder I just set up), along with some of the original photo-corners my mother used in my baby book, and I got to work on recreating my book of childhood highlights. I followed my mom's lead by adding insights and stories in my own handwriting to my "Happy Childhood" album, and I will continue to add pages as I have recollections that inspire me. Are you wondering about the photos that didn't make it into my album? They're waiting in my Storage Binder until I feel inspired to use them on additional layouts, which will go in my Library Albums. Just imagine the connections waiting to be discovered!

reality check

Attempting to sort, print, and store all of your pictures before moving forward is not a good idea. Instead, I recommend working in 5-year chunks, or purchasing a limited number of Storage Binders (perhaps no more than 10). This will keep things manageable, help you feel successful, and enable you to get back to creating layouts sooner. The energy you discover by using your newly established Library of Memories system will also fuel your efforts to introduce more pictures into it as you have room and time.

9 X 9 HAPPY CHILDHOOD ALBUM

trust me

You'll accomplish more in the task of sorting and storing if you snatch up small chunks of time over a period of several weeks than if you try to schedule a marathon session. Grab 15 minutes here and 30 minutes there, and you'll be amazed and energized by what you can get done.

I remember this house and the nubby brown sofa and my straight-legged dolly with shiny hair. I remember dressing up in mom's silky nightgown and feeling like a "fancy" lady. I absolutely remember my mom doing exercises with the man on the television (Jack LaLanne). I remember eating hot dogs and canned peaks with cottage cheese. I remember being tucked into bed and singing and laughing — happy memories.

JUNE 1969

Digital photos:
from camera to computer to prints

I'm usually pretty excited to browse through the photos I've uploaded to my computer. As I review each, frame by frame, I delete the shots I know I don't need (refer to the photo truths on page 44). I don't need images that are poorly composed, blurry, badly lit, or those that suffer from my lack of skill as a photographer—so I simply let them go!

My computer (specifically my iPhoto program) automatically sorts my digital photos chronologically by the date they were taken, so I don't have to spend time naming, labeling, or dating individual upload sessions. About every 3 months, I review all of the images I've uploaded into iPhoto and drag-and-drop those that I think I will *most* want to scrapbook into folders labeled with the appropriate season and year. (In iPhoto, this drag-and-drop step just makes a copy of the image, leaving the original in its chronological place.) This process allows me access to all of my images if I need to view them in order, and it helps separate out the best of the best so I can focus on printing, triaging, and scrapbooking. For example, after deleting the not-so-good images, I have 820 pictures left in iPhoto that were taken in January, February, and March of 2007. Of these, I dragged 311 "would love to scrapbook" images into my Winter 2007 folder.

reality check

Obviously, there's no way I'm going to scrapbook 311 pictures from Winter 2007 on actual layouts. After I upload my entire seasonal folder to a printing service, I further sift and select images to print. When I receive my prints, I temporarily house them in my Storage Binders so I can easily browse and select pictures when I am in "create mode." I'm fully aware that many photos I pay to print will eventually end up in Cold Storage or the trash can. For me, this calculated excess is not wasteful at all (*au contraire!*) because it means I have pictures at my fingertips when I'm ready to scrapbook. I consider these unused photo prints a small price to pay for productivity.

trust me

Since the advent of digital photography, your success as a scrapbooker depends on your ability to edit and categorize the sheer number of photos you take. You must decide which to upload and which to delete, which to move into working folders and which to print and store for future pages and projects. In my Winter 2007 example on the facing page, I moved less than half of the pictures I took into my working folder. That leaves 509 images behind. Now, you may be saying, "I could never do that!" But guess what? You absolutely need to if you are going to effectively deal with all of the pictures you take! The good news is you will get better and better at this sifting and editing process as you practice. And you will be a much happier scrapbooker for it.

CASE STUDY

From thirty to three

Even as cute as my little Addie is (I may be biased, but I'm
sure you'll agree), I can't possibly scrapbook every picture
I take of her. That means I shouldn't keep every photo
of her too, right? And I don't. For example, during a
February photo session, I took more than 30 pictures of
Addie. While that may seem like an almost-manageable
number, I knew I wouldn't (and couldn't) scrapbook all of
them—so I kept only 12 and put seven in my Winter 2007
folder. Much more doable than 30, don't you think?

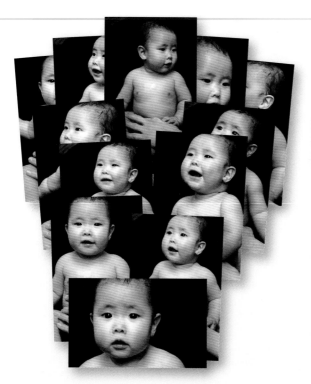

THESE PHOTOS MADE
THE FIRST CUT

THESE WENT INTO MY
WINTER 2007 FOLDER

love

you are six months old in this picture.

i am already 1,000 months in love.

THESE ARE THE THREE PHOTOS I USED ON MY 12 X 12 LAYOUT, WHICH WILL GO INTO MY ALL ABOUT ADDIE LIBRARY ALBUM

my
photos

what about ... instant gratification?

One of the advantages of digital technology is instant gratification. I love that I can immediately view my photos on my camera and quickly print them from my computer. So what happens when I want to create a layout with a photo I just snapped with my digital camera? I do it. Fresh pictures are often accompanied by fresh emotions and ideas and a sense of urgency for scrapbooking.

Please don't think I wait until the end of each season to print all of my pictures. (What a drag that would be!) I often order smaller batches of pictures, or print pictures at home. If and when there are leftovers in these small print orders, I generally file them directly into Category Drawers. On occasion, I'll print a whole batch of pictures (say, from a family reunion or vacation) and slip them into a Storage Binder almost immediately for use on current pages and projects. And when it comes time to print the remaining contents of that particular seasonal folder, I can generally remember what I have already printed so I don't order them again.

what about ... backing up digital images?

As fantastic as this digital age that we live in can be, there are also some risks associated with trusting a computer to keep all of your photos and memories safe. The thought is beyond sickening, but suppose your hard drive decides to crash tomorrow? (Take a deep breath and keep on reading; it's just a hypothetical.)

For starters, I recommend purchasing an external hard drive that will allow you to transfer files onto it at any time. Another option is burning photos onto CDs, sorted and labeled into folders just like those on your computer. To avoid loss as a result of a fire, flood, or other disaster, you may want to consider storing your back-up CDs out of your home. Another option to consider is an online photo service (like Shutterfly or Snapfish) that not only allows you to upload images for printing, but also saves your uploaded images forever. And I mean forever.

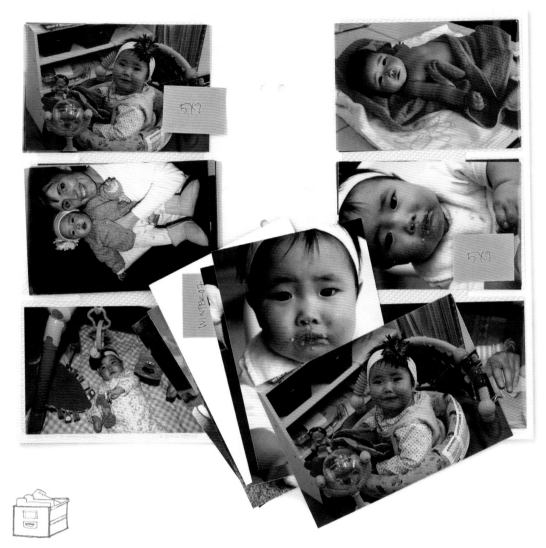

what about … enlargements?

Most of the time, I'm content scrapbooking standard 4 x 6 photos, but when I come across a really great image while placing a print order, I often choose to print an additional copy in the 5 x 7 size. Usually I don't know exactly how I'm going to use it—I just know I love it and won't mind having an extra copy to use in a big way.

When I'm slipping 4 x 6 prints into a Storage Binder and come across my enlargements, I place a sticky note on top of the photo sleeve to remind me that there is a 5 x 7 copy in one of my enlargement drawers. (I also add a sticky note to the back of my 5 x 7 print that tells me which Storage Binder contains

the corresponding 4 x 6 print.) I store my collection of ready-to-scrap enlargements in the same drawers where I keep heritage photos and documents (see page 31). In addition to the drawers labeled with individual names (for parents and grandparents), I have four enlargement drawers for portraits, people, places, and things. For example, a 5 x 7 print of Taft would go in the "people" enlargement drawer; one of the sunsets off my back porch goes in my enlargement drawer labeled "things."

Slipping new prints into Storage Binders

Once I've moved pictures from camera to computer and printed the ones I want to scrapbook someday, I slip them into Storage Binders. Here's a quick overview of how to tackle the job of sorting and storing your newly printed pictures in a Storage Binder:

1 **Start by making piles of related photos.** (For example, put all of the pictures from your weekend trip in one pile, all of the holiday pictures in another pile, and all of the random, everyday pictures in a third pile.)

2 **If you've ordered double prints or have multiple pictures** that are very similar, slip them into one album pocket or sleeve together. (I often stack four to six prints in one sleeve.)

3 **Don't worry about putting your prints in precise date order in your storage binder.** Close is good enough; it only takes a few minutes to flip through an entire storage binder to find the pictures you're looking for. (I promise, even if you don't scrapbook these photos for three years, knowing they're from Summer 2006 will be just as good as knowing they were taken on August 16, 2006.)

4 **Once you've slipped all of your prints into pockets, go back and add sticky notes with names or other specifics you're likely to forget.** If you'd like to, you can add to your to-do list any specific page or project ideas you have while putting the prints away. (And if you get inspired to stop and make a layout, do it!)

5 **Label or re-label the spine of your storage binder with the season and year** (I use my DYMO label maker for this). Add an additional label for major events (like a move, wedding, or vacation) that occurred during this time period. I don't note recurring events like birthdays and holidays, as I easily know which binder to grab when looking for those pictures.

6 **If you have lots of empty pocket pages in your Storage Binder** after you've stored away one season's prints, begin the next season in this same binder. If you only have a few empty pages, remove them so you can add them to other binders as needed.

trust me

You need to number the spines of your Storage Binders. This will help you put them back on the shelf in the proper order. My number labels go on the bottom of the album spine, and the date labels go on the top.

Photo Triage:
filling up your Category Drawers

"Photo triage" is a term my mother helped me invent many years ago. It is simply the process of removing a photo from its chronological context (i.e., Storage Albums) so you can see it in a different light, and eventually use it to make a connection that will enrich your scrapbooks. Category Drawers are intended to house a very small percentage of your overall photo collection—and these photos may live here for years and years—which allows you to naturally identify and ultimately illustrate patterns that are unique to your life. Once you have several years of photos viewable in Storage Albums, you can begin selecting a few to move and store in one of your four main Category Drawers: All About Us, People We Love, Places We Go, and Things We Do.

To give you an idea of what works for me, here's how I divide my four main categories into smaller subcategories:

In my US drawer there are eleven main tabs:

- **Together Forever**
  Pictures of two or more family members together, especially where there is a relationship shown.

- **All In The Family**
  Specifically for snapshots that feature my husband and me and all the kids.

- **Oh Brother**
  Pictures of two or more of my sons together, especially where there is a relationship shown.

- **Just The Girls**
  Pictures of me and Addie together, especially where our relationship is captured.

- **Seven Personality Tabs**
  I maintain one tab for each person in our immediate family, where I gather great shots depicting his or her individuality and personality. Behind each of these tabs I've set up a subcategory labeled, for example, "All About Chase," where I keep one or two pictures from birthdays and other milestone events in his life.

In my PEOPLE drawer there are three main tabs:

- **Grandparents**
  Pictures of, you guessed it, grandparents— with subcategories for each set of grandparents (e.g., Briggs & Connie Hall). I also have a subcategories called Grandma and Me and Grandpa and Me, where I store any pictures of a grandma or grandpa with one of my children.

- **Extended Family**
  Because I have a large extended family, I have subcategories for each of my husband's and my sibling's families (e.g., Theron & Kristin Hall or Amy & Dave Hoffman). I also have a tab labeled for our parents' families, where I store pictures of aunts, uncles, and cousins from each family.

- **Friends**
  Behind this main tab, you will find tabs for each person in my immediate family and their friends (e.g., Clark & Friends). I also have a tab for Family Friends (think Christmas card photos) and a tab labeled Teachers & Coaches.

In my PLACES drawer there are three main tabs:

- **Home**

  I have a subcategory for each different address we've called home (e.g., 2809 Melbourne). I also have a few other tabs for places like Grandma's House and the Backyard.

- **Near/Around Town**

  This is where I save pictures of locations and activities that are close to home—places like Riverfront Park, Dairy Queen, and Lake Coeur d'Alene.

- **Far Away**

  This tab is primarily for travel pictures, but I also have subcategories for Nature, and Ocean/Beach. Certain cities/vacation spots we have visited more than once (Seattle and Disneyland) have their own subcategory.

In my THINGS drawer there are five main tabs:

- **Everyday Life**

  I have 13 subcategories behind this tab—Animals/Pets, Bath Time, Camping, Cars, Computer, Eating, Food/Recipes, Hugs/Kisses/Smiles, Piano, Play, Read, Shoes, Sleep, and Treasures. Note: I also have lots of pictures stashed behind the main Everyday Life tab—these are snapshots that don't fit one of the above subcategories. I often "test out" new tabs in this drawer as our daily life changes. The trick is to not get so many individual tabs that you start to lose count!

- **Seasons and Colors**

  I keep subcategories for Winter, Spring, Summer, and Fall and Red, Orange, Yellow, Green, Blue, Purple, Brown, and Black/White.

- **Sports and Recreation**

  This holds subcategories for Baseball, Basketball, Soccer, Tae Kwon Do, Swimming, Hiking, Scooter, and Trampoline. A picture that doesn't fit in one of these subcategories (like bowling), simply gets placed behind the main tab.

- **Holidays and Traditions**

  With subcategories for Family Rituals, Valentines, St. Patrick's Day, Easter, 4th of July, Halloween/Costumes, Thanksgiving, and Christmas. Note: I place one, maybe two pictures taken at each annual holiday celebration behind these tabs. Others remain in my Storage Binders until they're scrapbooked!

- **Accomplishments**

  Here I have subcategories for Performances, School, Scouting, and Work. Other pictures of someone doing something exceptionally well, like riding a bike or tying shoes for the first time, are placed behind the main tab.

personal opinion

I do not attempt to triage pictures as I slip them into Storage Binders. Instead, I prefer to work fast, getting my prints in binders and then going back as time permits to thoughtfully move one or two at a time into my Category Drawers. Most of my triaging occurs later when I browse my Storage Binders in search of event-based pictures to scrapbook.

Initially, you may feel an urgency to get your Category Drawers filled up—but try to avoid this. Allow this collection of photos to grow organically over time.

Categorizing photos

Let's say you're flipping through your "Summer 2007" Storage Binder, ready to scrapbook pictures from a road trip you took in August, and you come across a single photo (of your child reading a book) you snapped a day or two after the trip. Since this photo is not tied to a specific event or particularly related to the season of summer, you could pull it out and file it in the Us drawer, behind that child's personality tab, or in the Things drawer behind Everyday Life or Reading.

Now, let's pretend you've just completed a layout about the road trip, and you have four pictures that didn't make it onto your page: ❶ This one is a near duplicate, and since the event has now been documented, you choose to toss it (refer to the photo truths on page 44). ❷ This is a picture of a friend relaxing at a rest stop, so you put it in your People We Love drawer behind the Friends tab. ❸ This extra shot of aspen trees with shimmering verdant leaves goes either in the Places drawer, behind the tab for Nature, or in the Things We Do drawer, behind the tab for Green. ❹ Lastly, there's a photo of you enjoying an ice cream cone. Since you love ice cream, this one could be triaged in the All About Us drawer, behind your personality tab. Or, if stopping for ice cream epitomizes summer road trips for you, then it could go in the Things We Do drawer behind Summer. It could also be filed in the Things We Do drawer behind a catch-all tab like Food/Eating. And finally, if the photo was taken in Redwood Forest, it could be filed behind the California tab in the Places We Go drawer.

The point here is that any one photo can be used to illustrate a number of different aspects of your life story. It's not important to know how you'll eventually use the photos you place in your Category Drawers. What's important is to set yourself up so you can make exciting connections and discover patterns that will feed your creativity in the future.

reality check

There are no hard and fast rules for where to file or triage a picture. There will likely be two or more tabs you could place it behind. Just go with your initial impression and remember the important thing is to "mix it up" so that you can see a photo in a new context. Don't stress about "losing" pictures or knowing exactly where they go—just relax and trust the process.

Category Drawers:
figuring out what goes where

Remember, what works for me may not necessarily work for you—especially when it comes to creating subcategories in your Category Drawers. To help you come up with tabs that truly represent the important people, places, and things in your life, consider the following questions:

People We Love Questions

1 Who are the people you will be scrapbooking regularly? (This list probably includes your immediate family members, but who else do you want to develop a character for in your ongoing scrapbook story?)

2 Who are your friends from childhood, college, work, church, etc.?

3 Who are the people in your neighborhood?

4 Who are the people you most admire in history?

5 Who are the people in pop culture, politics, or your personal areas of interest that inspire you?

Places We Go Questions

1 Where have you lived in your life? Where do you live now?

2 What places are part of your family heritage?

3 What places have you visited while on vacation?

4 What places do you hope to visit someday?

5 What places do you associate with learning or personal development?

6 Where do you go on a weekly, monthly, or yearly basis?

7 What places in your home (or the homes of loved ones) do you associate with special memories?

a note

Most people (myself included) don't automatically take the kinds of pictures that will visually contribute to an authentic scrapbook story. I've discovered that by generating these kinds of lists, I can recognize the photo opportunities that will be the most meaningful to me.

Things We Do Questions

1. What have been the milestones and defining events of your life thus far?

2. What skills or experiences led you to your life's work?

3. What aspects of nature do you love the most?

4. What do you do to recharge or motivate yourself?

5. What are your personal treasures?

6. What do you collect or spend money on over and over?

7. What unexpected challenges or surprises in life have given you a cause?

8. What things do you see or encounter that remind you of specific people?

9. What everyday activities could be used to describe your life now and in times past?

All About Us Questions

Ask each member of your immediate family to answer the following questions:

1. What is your favorite color?

2. What are your favorite foods?

3. How do you most like to spend your time?

4. What is something you do really well?

5. What are some compliments people frequently give you?

6. What is your best memory from the last year?

7. What is your best quality or personality trait?

8. What is something you are working on or have accomplished that makes you proud?

9. What makes you special and unique?

Photo Triage in action: making sense of the process

To help you better understand the variety of pictures and kaleidoscope of memories that are brought together through the process of photo triage, let's take a peek into the contents of my category drawers. Under each picture, I've noted when it was taken and where it can be found now. By simply removing a photo from its chronological reference, you unleash its potential to speak to timeless aspects of your life—primarily personalities and relationships, but also the changing and unchanging nature of your everyday life. From my experience, triaged pictures are hidden gems— invaluable in helping us tell our most important (read: priceless) stories.

TAKEN: JULY 4TH, 2006
DRAWER: THINGS WE DO
SUB-CATEGORY/TAB: HOLIDAYS/4TH OF JULY

TAKEN: GEOF'S BIRTHDAY TRIP, MAY 2006
DRAWER: PEOPLE WE LOVE
SUB-CATEGORY/TAB: FRIENDS/FAMILY FRIENDS

TAKEN: GEOF'S BIRTHDAY TRIP, MAY 2006
DRAWER: PLACES WE GO
SUB-CATEGORY: NATURE

TAKEN: ADDIE'S TEMPLE SEALING, MAY 2007
DRAWER: ALL ABOUT US
SUB-CATEGORY: TOGETHER FOREVER

TAKEN: AFTER SHOPPING AT COSTCO, JUNE 2007
DRAWER: THINGS WE DO
SUB-CATEGORY: EVERYDAY LIFE

TAKEN: VALENTINES' DAY, 2004
DRAWER: ALL ABOUT US
SUB-CATEGORY: OH BROTHER

TAKEN: AT A HARVEST FAIR, SEPTEMBER 2007
DRAWER: THINGS WE DO
SUB-CATEGORY/TAB: SEASONS/FALL

TAKEN: EASTER SUNDAY, 2007
DRAWER: ALL ABOUT US
SUB-CATEGORY: OH BROTHER

TAKEN: ON A GIRLS' WEEKEND,
APRIL 2006
DRAWER: PEOPLE WE LOVE
SUB-CATEGORY/TAB:
EXTENDED FAMILY/CHANDA
& JON SEITER

TAKEN: AFTER CHURCH
IN JUNE 2006
DRAWER: PEOPLE WE LOVE
SUB-CATEGORY/TAB:
GRANDPARENTS/GRANDMA
AND ME

TAKEN: BEFORE EASTER 2005
DRAWER: THINGS WE DO
SUB-CATEGORY/TAB: COLORS/GREEN

TAKEN: AT LUNCH WHILE SCHOOL
SHOPPING WITH CLARK, SEPT 2006
DRAWER: THINGS WE DO
SUB-CATEGORY/TAB: EVERYDAY LIFE/FOOD

Cold Storage:
cleaning out your Storage Binders

I only store pictures in my Storage Binders if I think I might want to scrapbook them. Storage Binders are intended to be active, temporary working files that allow me to become familiar with my pictures, be inspired to scrapbook or triage them, and be able to prioritize them as time passes. To keep things manageable, I've limited my collection of Storage Binders to 15, which means that in order to make room for current pictures, I have to condense the contents of my binders and occasionally remove pictures altogether. If photos have lived in my Storage Binders for 4 or more years, and in that time I have not been inspired to scrapbook them or triage them into my Category Drawers, I move them to inactive Cold Storage. Pictures in Cold Storage can still be revisited and retrieved, but they do not bog down the flow of current photos. This survival of the fittest approach to my photos helps me stay on top of my scrapbooking without getting overwhelmed by the number of photos at my fingertips.

personal opinion

I don't spend a lot of time organizing photos in my Cold Storage boxes. (OK, I don't spend ANY time organizing photos in my Cold Storage boxes.) Last time I checked, there were far more interesting and engaging things to do. When I move pictures to Cold Storage, I lift up the lid to the most recent box and put the photos in the front. No tabs, no intentional date order—just a wonderful feeling of "Ah, that's out of my way for now!"

five

Dealing with memorabilia

I feel 100 percent secure in my assumption that you have a backlog of memory-laden stuff that isn't pictures—things you want to include in your scrapbooks. I bring home tickets, maps, guides, and brochures from vacations, exhibits, and programs. I cut articles from newspapers and magazines, and I dutifully save meaningful cards, letters, and certificates. I almost never exercise restraint when I am in collecting mode, and I probably don't need to tell you that my appetite for collecting parallels my appetite for taking photos! For years, these bits and pieces used to get lost in the shuffle, only to resurface after the relevant photos had been scrapbooked. (See, I do understand!) I'm now learning to develop a critical filter for what to save and what to let go, and this ability to edit has enabled me to track and use memorabilia more often and in more meaningful ways on my pages. I have three main strategies for storing and retrieving memorabilia:

1 **Oversize zipper bags (for travel/vacation memorabilia)**

When I return from a trip, I put everything I gathered into a large plastic bag. When I print and slip my vacation/travel photos into Storage Binders, I add a sticky note that says something like, "don't forget the stuff!" (I may or may not be more specific than that.) When I eventually move any unscrapped travel photos out of Storage Binders and into Cold Storage, I locate and toss any unused memorabilia—reminding myself that if I haven't used it yet, it's time to part with it.

2 **Memorabilia Notebook**

I have a binder filled with planner sheets and page protectors where I save a small collection of everyday stuff that is truly valuable to specific events or moments. I only put memorabilia in this preparatory binder if I am 98 percent sure I will use it. I revisit this binder often as a "start here" for creating pages. For more about my Memorabilia Notebook, see page 22.

3 **Cultural Memorabilia Box**

I've set aside a drop-and-go container that holds the smaller and more random tidbits that I save. The wrappers, tags, labels, paint swatches, and other miscellaneous items I collect here are more likely to serve as layout accents than as the foundation for a layout. I love my little suitcase-style box, and the contents add an authentic texture to my pages that pictures alone simply cannot! See page 32 for more about my Cultural Memorabilia Box.

don't forget the stuff!

what about ... crops?

If you're like many of your fellow scrapbookers, you don't always scrapbook at home. Sometimes you like to take your creativity on the road to an organized crop or a casual gathering with a few friends. While it's fun to scrapbook with others, you may feel overwhelmed at the thought of prepping for an away-from-home scrapbooking adventure. (What will you feel like creating? What materials and photos should you bring? How can you possibly haul *everything* you might need?)

It's hard to prep and create away from home, but you can easily visit with friends (and eat chocolate) while you work on certain Library of Memories tasks, such as:

- Updating an ongoing project or album with the help of a Materials File

- Slipping photos into a Storage Binder

- Square punching pictures from a Cold Storage box

- Sorting and labeling digital images on your laptop

reality check

Most scrapbookers I know head to a 6-hour crop with two or *more* pull totes, each exceeding the weight limit allowed on a jumbo jet. If you want to experience a true sense of power when packing for a crop, grab an album you want to update or finish, your materials file, some chocolate (of course!), and a basic tool kit. If by chance you realize you've forgotten something, you can use your chocolate in negotiations to acquire it.

Library Albums:
categorizing your finished albums

To get started scrapbooking, all you need at first is four empty albums, one each for Places We Go, Things We Do, People We Love, and All About Us. (Notice that these are the same titles you applied to your Category Drawers.) As you complete a layout, determine which album it goes in and slip it in! Don't worry about chronology. Just slip them into an album as you complete them. If you decide later that a layout belongs in a different album, no worries. Layouts are portable!

As you start filling up your Library Albums, you'll want to apply framework pages to those albums to help keep your layouts organized. By framework pages I mean *title pages* and *section pages*. A great place to start is to just copy the main tabs in each of your four Category Drawers. For example, my Places We Go album has the same three sections that my Category Drawers have: Home, Around Town, and Far Away. At first, all of these sections fit nicely inside one album, but now I have two full Places We Go albums—one that includes Home and Around Town, and one that features

Far Away layouts. I absolutely love the flexibility of my albums because they can grow and change as my family does, and they are totally independent of chronology!

To bring additional structure to my library, my title pages and section pages all follow a consistent look and feel. For example, the title page for my Things We Do album features a photo that represents (to me) the overall contents of the album. The background of the layout is the same color of pink as the album cover (I stock up on cardstock that matches my albums), but I've also added touches of the other three colors (green, red, and brown) to connect this album with my other Library Albums. My section pages follow a different design scheme: they're all one color, and they feature photos that are specific to that subcategory's theme (see page 77).

COLORS ♥ SEASONS

subcategory's theme (see page 77).

Once you select and purchase Library Albums and start filling them with layouts, you can begin creating your title pages and section pages. But don't feel like you *have* to create them right away. Finding photos for these pages will be easier if you've already made some progress filling up your Category Drawers—and that takes time. In other words, when I created my Things We Do title page, I simply went to my Things We Do drawer and pulled out photos I wanted to use. Photos for my Everyday Life section page were easily retrieved from behind my Everyday Life tab.

trust me

Trust me, in time you will get it. This organizational system will soon become second nature to you—a process that you engage in automatically, a process that allows you the freedom to respond to the inspiration that's all around you.

Growing your library

The more you scrapbook, the faster your Library Albums will fill up. When you have filled one of your initial Library Albums with completed layouts, determine which section you will move to a new album. The section page will become the title page of the new album, and you will have opened up needed space in both of these albums. Don't stress about the specifics of growing your library in the beginning—it all just happens naturally; where you have one album now, you'll eventually have an extended set of albums. In my world, the All About Us albums grow most quickly, both because I tend to create more pages about my immediate family and because I keep adding children! I originally had one All About Us album with sections for three boys. Each of those section pages has now become a title page that introduces an entire album dedicated to each boy. And when those albums fill up, I begin volume two.

what about … page size?

Originally, layouts for my Library Albums were all 8½ x 11, but when I upgraded to the albums I use now, I was able to add a 12 x 12 album to each of my four main categories. This has given me the freedom to create layouts in both sizes and still have a place to store them. Some album styles may even accommodate different layout sizes in the same album. Think about how you can leave yourself open to lots of options. Creative freedom is a very good thing!

trust me

Keep the design of your framework pages simple and easy to duplicate—and by all means, use products and supplies that you can stockpile. You'll thank me later!

TITLE PAGE

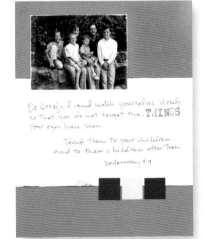

DEDICATION PAGE

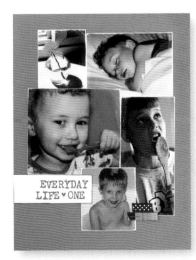

SECTION PAGE

SECTION PAGE

TRY THIS!

Start Here Jar

When I have 15 minutes to spend scrapbooking and I have no idea where to start, I turn to my Start Here jar for some creative direction. All I have to do is grab a Popsicle stick and follow the instructions written on it. If the stick says "Places We Go," then I turn to that Category Drawer to find photos and ideas for a layout. If it says "digital triage," I spend my fifteen minutes organizing photos and uploading them for printing. Get the idea? It's a fun, simple way to maximize whatever time I have for scrapbooking—and it's tied to the memory-based way my photos are organized.

To create your own Start Here jar, gather the following items:

- One small container (a jar or soup can will do)
- Scraps of patterned paper and ribbon you love
- Rub-on letters
- Sixteen Popsicle sticks
- Black pen

Then write the following phrases on the end of your Popsicle sticks:

- All About Us (on two sticks)
- People We Love (on two sticks)
- Places We Go (on two sticks)
- Things We Do (on two sticks)
- Storage Albums (on two sticks)
- Theme Albums/Materials File
- Photos I Love (see page 90)
- Family Words File
- Cultural Memorabilia Box
- Digital Triage

reality check

Be honest, your creative urges are often frustrated by the idea that you need to scrapbook the next chronological set of photos, right? Who wants to scrapbook back-to-school if you just purchased gorgeous paisley and plaid papers that remind you of your sister? It's time to break out of that mind set and follow where inspiration leads!

start here

Places We Go

All About Us

Theme Album

Pages & projects: where the photos originated

In the pages that follow, I'll share several of my recent pages and projects, along with the story of how my Library of Memories system made them possible.

At this point, you might be saying to yourself, "It's about time! I thought this girl was all about simplifying; all *I* wanted to do was scrapbook!" Please remember that my system has evolved over the course of many years and that it may take some time for you to feel comfortable with the processes I've shared with you. But, as these projects will prove, it is worth it!

Remember, too, that the ultimate goal is not confusion and busy work, but clarity and productivity—it's about getting you to a place where you can scrapbook for fun because you feel inspired to do so.

trust me

Trust me, you don't have to track and match up perfectly all the bits and pieces that make up your stories. This isn't rocket science. When it comes to remembering and preserving the patterns and rituals that make us unique, *close* is definitely good enough.

CASE STUDY
Grandma Addie

In a recent email from *storypeople.com* (I'm signed up for the company's daily messages), I read a quote that made me think of my Grandma Addie and how much I miss her. I put the email in my "save" folder and made a mental note to use it on a layout and include images from her home. Later that same week, I came across several Fourth of July pictures I had printed for a 6 x 6 album that never happened, including a "mistake print" of my grandma's face. (Somehow the photo came back cropped much tighter than I wanted for that album.) I'm so glad I saved this photo, because it jumped out at me as the perfect illustration for the quote I had saved.

I dropped what I was doing and immediately went to my Places drawer, behind the Grandma's House subcategory tab, to find pictures of her house and yard. An hour later, I had a completed layout to add to our People We Love album in the Grandparents section. This process of acting on a memory trigger, *and* being able to stumble upon and gather appropriate photos, is a perfect example of how my Library of Memories system supports inspiration-based scrapbooking. It's a powerful feeling to find what you need while the emotion is fresh. I *love* my Category Drawers!

I buried a nickle under the porch when I was 8, she said, but one day my grandma died and they sold the house and I never got to go back for it. A nickel used to mean something, I said. She nodded. It stiel does, she said and then she started to cry.

Tooth fairy tales

While flipping through my Memorabilia Binder one day, I came across these hilarious notes two of my sons wrote to the tooth fairy, and then I remembered seeing some new tooth fairy stickers in my product stash. For me, that was all the inspiration I needed to find some pictures (in my Us drawer behind the All About Chase and All About Trey tabs) and create a page about our family's communication with the elusive little tooth fairy!

Please note, I didn't actually use photos taken at the same time my boys wrote their letters. It's okay to combine notes and photos from different dates—and it's okay to highlight two boys on the same page.

This page is a great illustration of the power of a Memorabilia Binder. When you tuck something like a handwritten tooth fairy note away into your Binder, you buy yourself some time to collect other items (in this case, an additional note!). When you're ready, you can simply pair the memorabilia with relevant (notice I didn't say matching) photos. And, yes, there are actual Julian teeth in that little envelope—but there's a very good chance that they don't even belong to these two boys (and that's okay too—as long as you don't tell them).

Poolside pictures

While browsing my Summer 2005 storage binder, I came across some poolside pictures taken during a trip to San Diego. I pulled out five or six, thinking I would make a quick page with just those photos. When I started moving things around, I decided I would definitely not be using two of the pictures—so on my way to grab blue embellishments, I decided to drop those two pictures behind the Swimming tab in my Things drawer. It sounds funny, but that proved to be the critical move for this layout. While filing my two photos in the drawer, I found four pictures of Clark (much younger than he is now) that I had recently reintroduced into my categories from Cold Storage. They stopped me in my tracks, and a bunch of random memories flooded in. I felt inspired to switch gears. I still ended up with a swim page, but it is far more meaningful than what I had originally intended.

personal opinion

I think one of the reasons scrapbookers say, "I'm just not very creative," is because they confuse creativity with finished pages. Creativity is much more about process than outcome, and in order to really discover creativity in yourself, you need to allow ideas to evolve.

CASE STUDY

Birthday boy

This page is an example of how I scrapbook events. I took tons of photos at Taft's 6th birthday party. After uploading and deleting, I kept 68 digital birthday images in my iPhoto library, moved 32 images into my Spring 2007 folder, and later printed 25 for scrapbooking, filing them away in a Storage Binder labeled "Spring 2007." When I eventually was inspired to scrapbook the event, I quickly pulled out the prints, made the page, and filed the leftovers in three places: my Category Drawers, a Cold Storage box, and my circular file (a.k.a. trash can). Only nine of the 25 likely-to-be-scrapped photos in my Storage Binder made it onto my layout. Six more are sitting in Category Drawers waiting to be rediscovered, and I decided to simply let go of the rest.

Here's exactly where the leftovers ended up:

① Close-up photo of the cake
Things drawer/Food tab

② Two additional birthday pictures
Us drawer/All About Taft tab (one shown)

③ Photo of Clark in a tree
Us drawer/Clark Personality tab

④ Picture of the dragon and cake
Things drawer/Color tab/Green subcategory tab

⑤ Photo of Taft and Cody
People drawer/Taft Friends tab

⑥ Two extra birthday pictures
Cold Storage (not pictured)

On average, I'm probably only scrapbooking 15 percent of the pictures I take, but I am scrapbooking! Please don't let the sheer number of pictures you have prevent you from documenting the days you don't want to forget.

trust me

I know it can be a scary thing to intentionally remove pictures from chronological order and file them into Category Drawers. You wonder if you will somehow lose them; you fret about forgetting the details of when and where they were taken. But it's okay! Keep the end goal in mind. You're setting yourself up to find, in a matter of seconds, pictures that go together—not because they were taken together, but because they tell the story of family, friendship, personality, and perspective. That's some seriously good stuff!

one	dragon themed birthday party
two	hours jammed-packed with fun
three	brothers that helped pull it off
four	activities including pin the fire on the dragon, kill the dragon {piñata,} rescue the princess and become an honorary knight
five	friends that came to celebrate and play
six	a very good number to be!!

6

You make me smile

CASE STUDY

Clark's friends

Category Drawers are the coolest! You may have to experience what they do firsthand before you can really buy into their importance. This page is a great illustration of how my Category Drawers enhance my scrapbooking and save me a ton of time.

Clark entered high school this year, and we've talked a lot about his friends and how important it is to find good friends that you can trust. As soon as I took on this book assignment, I knew I wanted to create a big 12 x 12 spread featuring Clark's friends from the last 14 years. Of course I stayed up late working on it—but when I showed it to Clark the next morning, he spent several minutes looking at the pictures and then said, "Wow, this is pretty much everybody! Nice job, Mom."

Sure, I could've created this layout without Category Drawers—but it would've taken me a *long* time to track down pictures of every friend my son has had. I probably would've had to hunt through boxes and boxes of chronologically sorted photos just to make one page. But thanks to my Category Drawers, I could quickly round up a collection of photos from various years (and impress my teenager in the process).

a note

To add a personal touch to the layout, I asked Clark to list the names of his friends in his own handwriting.

Create t-shirt

I loved making this layout, probably because it's all about creating. Here's the story: my friend Trina gave me a fun, long-sleeved T-shirt that I loved and wore quite frequently—at least, until I got a big ink stain right on the front. (Darn!) Before throwing it out, I cut out the word "create" from the shirt and tossed it into my Cultural Memorabilia Box, with no idea of how and when I would use it. In the meantime, I started listening to a series of podcasts about creativity, and I was thinking about how to scrapbook some of my feelings on the subject. The next time I opened my memorabilia box, I saw the shirt scrap and knew it was time to add it to a page. Behind the All About Stacy tab in my Us drawer, I found the photo of me (appropriately) taken at a scrapbooking workshop. Easy as that, I had the makings of an authentic layout!

trust me

When you're willing to accept who you are, embrace your unique perspective, and tackle obstacles to your creative process, you *will* be able to share your life stories in colorful and meaningful ways—you will be scrapstrong!

CASE STUDY

Page in progress

Electronics Today—sounds like the name of a geeky technology journal, huh? It's also going to be a layout in the Everyday Life section of my Things We Do album very soon. You see, not too long ago, Trey came bursting into my office and said he *had* to talk to me. He then went on to describe with much animation a new table invention that can display photos and even download them from your phone and camera. While I'm unable to verify this, I can say that we went on to imagine together what his world might be like when he's a grown-up. It all made me think about how fast technology is changing and how very much it touches our everyday lives.

After that fun chat with Trey, I was inspired to gather some pictures (from my Things

drawer behind the Computer tab and from each of my sons' tabs in my Us drawer). I also found a portion of a Radio Shack ad that I'd cut out of the newspaper and tossed into my Cultural Memorabilia Box. (And I'm holding off for one of those Target electronics fliers that go out before the holidays—to help me document all the gadgets that are a part of our world today.) Although I haven't yet created this page, it is on my to-do list!

a note

I generally don't pre-plan pages by gathering scrapbook products, but I do occasionally pull pictures together and store them in 8 x 8 page protectors. Even then, I don't like having more than three such pages in progress waiting for me at one time.

15-minute fixes

Let's face it. Sometimes it's a miracle to squeeze 15 spare minutes out of a busy day. But instead of waiting for the far-off day when you'll be able to sit down and scrapbook for hours on end, start with 15 minutes here and there. Set a timer and see how much you can actually accomplish in that time. Not sure where to start? Here's a short list:

- Download images from your camera to your computer

- Review and tag digital images

- Upload a folder of images for online storage and printing

- Back up digital images onto an external hard drive or compact disk

- Slip photo prints into a Storage Binder

- Browse through a Storage Binder and triage a few photos into Category Drawers

- Pull photos from a Storage Binder or Category Drawer and place them on your work table with cardstock and other paper you might want to use to scrapbook them

- File completed layouts into Library Albums

- Create a title or section page

- Sit down with a family member and enjoy completed layouts in your library

All of these tasks are quick, 15-minute projects that you may not consider traditional scrapbooking, but they are. The more you accomplish in short spurts, the more energy you'll have for the creative process of assembling layouts.

IN 15 MINUTES, YOU CAN CREATE A TITLE OR SECTION PAGE FOR ONE OF YOUR ALBUMS

trust me

I know the exhaustion of being a mom and working full time. If I take 15 minutes at the start of my day to lay out some photos and paper, and these are "on my mind" all day, I'm much more likely to want to return after the kids are in bed.

CASE STUDY

Photos I love

If you've read either of my previous books, you know I believe in starting and maintaining a Photos I Love album to showcase your most beloved photos (which, by the way, are not necessarily your "best" photos). These are the pictures that elicit in you an "ahhh" response and carry extraordinary emotional connections. I have an ongoing Photos I Love album, and I've recently begun a mini-library of five 8 x 8 Photos I Love albums, one for each of my children, where I collect my favorite pictures of them as they grow up. Before I add finished pages to their albums, I display them on their bedroom doors in cool acrylic frames. (My teenage boys give me a hard time, but I know they love it!) Pictures for these frames and albums generally come from my All About Us drawer behind my kids' personality tabs. Sometimes I include a story or experience from their lives or write a letter to them expressing feelings and advice. Other times I don't journal at all.

These five albums are stored in a sofa table in our living room, where I can catch a glimpse of their colorful spines. (There is just something so energizing about incorporating the evidence of what I do into my family's everyday environment!)

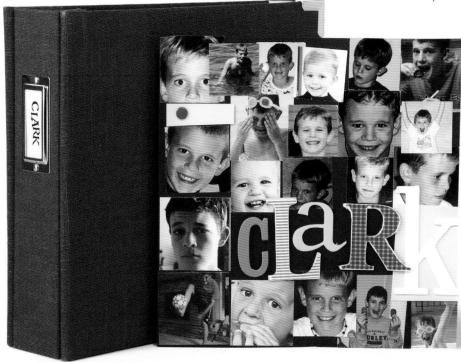

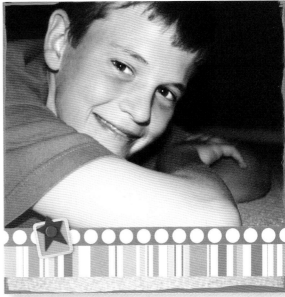

But what I really want you to know about this project is the way it uses two of the extras we talked about in chapter one.

- When my kids get to be high-school age, like Clark, I'm going to create official title pages for their Photos I Love albums by combining a bunch of square-punched face photos. And where will those photos come from? My Square-Punch Picture Drawers, of course! (see page 37)

- The closing page of each Photos I Love album, titled "famous last words," features two quotes pulled from my Family Words File (see page 34) and one personality picture.

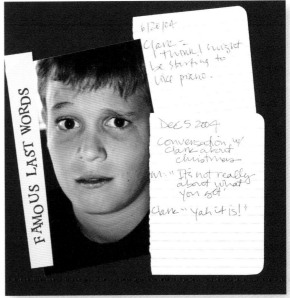

Can you image having an album like this highlighting the life of someone you love or admire? What a treasure! I'm pretty sure I'll send these Photos I Love albums off to live with my children when they leave, but as always I'm reserving the right to change my mind.

what about ... you?

The Photos I Love concept is one of the most versatile I know. I've centered mine on my five children—but if you don't have children, why not create a four-album collection of seasonal photo favorites (each dedicated to a season of the year)? To do this, simply set up tabs labeled winter, spring, summer, and autumn in your Things drawer. Are you a traveler? How cool would it be to do a similar Photos I Love collection with four albums, designated north, south, east, and west—featuring pictures from your travels to all four corners of the earth?

personal opinion

The science of positive psychology has proven that surrounding ourselves and our families with positive images is healing. According to educational psychologist Ruth Richards, images are a special language that can enhance and "...in some cases restore mental, emotional, or spiritual capacities." Wow. What do you say we display our favorite photos before tucking them away in albums!

To set up your own Photos I Love kid edition, you'll need:

- A small album for each child (I chose each kid's favorite color)

- Acrylic page frames to display pages before they are filed away

- A growing collection of personality pictures, from which you can select your favorites

- Square-Punch Picture Drawers (with pictures inside)

- A Family Words File

- Time and patience (no need to rush this project—the longer it takes, the more authentic the memories and insights will be)

CASE STUDY

Hanging tag books

Not long ago, I found a functional piece of home décor that's perfect for my kitchen and family. It features seven little chalkboards (one for every day of the week) with a hook beneath each. I was unsure what to do with the hooks until I posted a picture on my blog and someone gave me the idea to create mini-albums all about each person in my family. (And how convenient is it that there are seven of us?)

One of my favorite things to do is set up a scheme for a scrapbook project and customize it to fit different people or situations. Here's the outline I'm following and adapting for my kitchen tag books:

- cover image
- birth date and place
- baby photo
- one or two personality photos
- personal statement or quote
- one or two personality photos
- "lives to" list
- one or two photos depicting items from this list
- "known for" list
- one or two photos depicting qualities from this list
- back cover image

I probably don't need to tell you this again, but pictures for this kind of project are a snap to pull together if you have Category Drawers. I used photos from the individual personality tabs in my Us drawer. (See page 62 for a review of my categories and subcategories.)

movie Night

trust me

Not every memory you preserve must end up in your Library Albums. Please allow your system to support all of your creative goals, from card-making to home décor to mini-albums. And don't you think these albums would look equally adorable stashed in a big basket or displayed on a shelf?

CASE STUDY

Photos from London

I'm not bent on scrapbooking all of my photos in the same way. When I end up with hundreds of photos from a trip or other experience, I can fuel several pages and projects and really appreciate the unique ideas and perspectives that spring from each one. In April 2007, I had the amazing opportunity to travel to London (to teach scrapbooking, of course!), and I decided to bring my mother (or mum) along. Follow along as I outline what I've created so far with the piles of pictures I took on that trip.

1 After initially uploading and deleting the no-good shots, I had 235 images in my library. I moved 157 into my Spring 2007 folder and eventually printed the whole folder.

2 From there, I used seven images to highlight my London adventures on a two-page spread for our Places We Go album, under the Far Away section.

a note

Turn the page to see some of the pages from my photo album scrapbook.

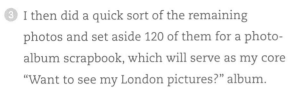 I then did a quick sort of the remaining photos and set aside 120 of them for a photo-album scrapbook, which will serve as my core "Want to see my London pictures?" album.

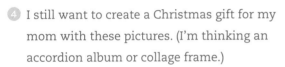 I still want to create a Christmas gift for my mom with these pictures. (I'm thinking an accordion album or collage frame.)

where does it all go?

This album will be kept out on display in our music and memory room—I am planning on taking it to Thanksgiving this year so I can share my experiences with extended family. Did I mention, liberating?

London tower...

...it All HappeneD Here...

And more!

Amazing ArcHitecture and History At every turn.

unbelievAble sigHts

PHOTO ALBUM SCRAPBOOKING HAS REALLY BROADENED MY DEFINITION OF SCRAPBOOKING

photo album scrapbooking

For some reason, most of us have the idea that using a photo album to store and share photos is a cop out, like it's a lesser form of scrapbooking because it doesn't require as much time or creativity as making layouts. Wrong! Not only are photo albums OK to use, they can become your best friend. If you let them, photo albums can relieve you of the burden of hundreds of pictures that you really don't want to use on layouts—and they can help you easily document your memories during times when life is especially demanding. If you're feeling burdened by hundreds of baby pictures of your now 12-year-old, compile them into a photo album scrapbook, and enjoy the wonderful feeling of losing that baby weight!

THIS BLUE-DOOR PHOTO, TAKEN IN LONDON, INSPIRED ME TO CREATE A "TRAVEL INSPIRATION" CHIPBOARD JOURNAL WHERE I'LL DISPLAY FAVORITE IMAGES FROM ALL MY FAVORITE DESTINATIONS

personal opinion

Anytime you pair a photo with a memory, you are scrapbooking. This means scrapbooks come in all shapes and sizes. Ten or 15 years ago, it made sense to funnel your photos through the same process and create a complete collection of 12 x 12 layouts. With so many additional options available today, limiting yourself to just one page size, destined for one type of album, would be like going to the buffet and eating only the mashed potatoes. You gotta love mashed potatoes, but they're really so much better when surrounded by other foods and flavors. I encourage you to take off the blinders and dish up something new!

CASE STUDY

Happy colors

When I feel like being creative but don't have a particular project in mind, I often pick up my *Big Picture* tag book* and flip through it for inspiration. One particular evening, I got to the happy colors page in my tag book and thought, "Hey, maybe that's what I should start now." And when I glanced up at my inspiration board in my studio to see the colorful socks postcard, that was all it took. I decided to make a mini-book with that whimsical image on the cover!

The pictures came from my Things drawer behind individual color tabs. I completed each mini-collage with a few embellishments from my color drawers (where I store my products, organized by color), adding a Pantone swatch or two for continuity. Setting up a text box on my computer made the journaling a snap. The whole project came together in two evenings. It sits on a shelf in my studio, next to a big jar of jelly beans, and it definitely makes me happy!

Cover postcard from Little Miss Matched

(littlemissmatched.com)

*My *Big Picture* tag book is included in the back of my book, *The Big Picture, Scrapbook Your Life and a Whole Lot More*

100

trust me

Trust me when I say my system isn't perfect. I'm continually looking for ways to make things easier and more efficient. I first wrote about a library approach to scrapbooking in my book *Simple Scrapbooks* (published by *Creating Keepsakes* magazine in December 2000), and while my system is still the same at the core, it has been through countless iterations and upgrades. In fact, I have very recently added brand-new elements (like my Square-Punch Picture Drawers shown on page 37) and renamed and refashioned others (like my title pages and Family Tree Drawers). I've been at this for a long time, so trust me and trust yourself. As you push ahead, determined to be flexible and embracing opportunities to try new ideas, you will discover how to use and adapt what I do to fit your own life and scrapbooking goals.

people

WE LOVE

things that Matter

chapter
3

Your results

I'm sure it's obvious by now that I *love* my Library of Memories
system. (If it's not, maybe you need to go back and read chapters
1 and 2 again!) This system absolutely works for me, and I know
it can work for you too. But you don't have to take my word for it.
In the pages that follow, you'll hear from a group of scrapbookers
who've adopted my system and made it their own.

In this chapter...

- You'll meet scrapbookers who, perhaps just like you,
  have let their obligation to chronology drive
  (and even dilute) their scrapbooking.

- You'll discover a variety of adaptations
  to my system—adaptations that may
  work for you, or at least get you
  moving toward your own unique approach.

- You'll find that the only right way to apply this
  system to your hobby is the way that fits your
  goals, budget, and lifestyle.

chapter 3: preview

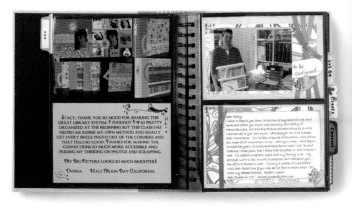

You may be wondering how it's possible

that other scrapbookers have implemented my system, considering that this book is supposed to be an introduction to it. Well, I teach an online Library of Memories class through *bigpicturescrapbooking. com*, so I've had a chance to test out the system on hundreds of scrapbookers already. In my class, I walk students through everything I've just shared with you—the three essentials, the nine extras, and how they all work together to enable inspiration-based scrapbooking.

Each person who signs up for the class comes for a different reason. Many are (beyond) burned out on the hobby they once loved; some are confused about how to stay creative in their "get caught up" mindset. And others are simply looking for ways to make scrapbooking meaningful again. Any of those reasons sound familiar?

How about these?

"I felt I was going in circles, organizing my photos, but never knowing where anything was, or how to get started. I felt I had to go year by year and I was just so behind. "

MAUREEN SARGENT, DEDHAM, MASSACHUSETTS

"I was constantly caught in the whirlwind of the next new technique or product rather than scrapbooking quickly, creatively, and in a functional way."

NARELLE JURSS, PERTH, AUSTRALIA

"I was trying to scrapbook chronologically. It constantly left me feeling behind, guilty, frustrated, and overwhelmed—to the point where I was seriously disillusioned, lacking direction, and wondering if scrapbooking was actually worth the angst. This is meant to be a pleasurable hobby after all!"

RACHELLE HARVEY, MOSS VALE, NEW SOUTH WALES, AUSTRALIA

At the conclusion of a recent 16-week Library of Memories class, I was thrilled to receive a special memento from a group of students—a photo album packed with photos and notes about how adapting my system has brought inspiration back into their scrapbooking. As I thumbed through its pages, I realized how important it is for you to know that implementing the Library of Memories system does not mean copying my system. You can adapt it to fit your life and your hobby.

And that's why I want to introduce you to 13 women who, after taking my Library of Memories class, modified my approach so it suits their own unique needs. They've adapted my ideas, tossed out the pieces that don't work for them, and added new elements that better fit their lifestyles. As you will see, these women are just like you: they have a deep desire to scrapbook what matters most to them in a fun, inspiring way—without throwing their lives out of balance in the process. Drum roll, please!

Start Here

Start Again

Melanie Sidaro

Dear Stacy-
Thank you for the inspiration
and guida...
during th...
I will th...
pull a sti...
jar. This...
way of li...
continually...

STACY, THANK YOU SO MUC...
GREAT LIBRARY SYSTEM. I T...
ORGANIZED AT THE BEGINN...
HELPED ME REFINE MY OW...
GET EVERY SINGLE PHOTO...
THAT FEELS SO GO...
CONNECTIONS SO...
FREEING MY THINK...

MY BIG PICT...

...class...
...therapy for scrapbookers.
I feel in
control of
my hobby,
and that makes
me so very happy.
Thank you

Stacy-
Thank you so much for...
your vision with us. You...
had a profound influence...
...otos I take...

Leave behind the constraints
& guilt associated with
chronological scrapbooking.

Stacy,
I can't thank you enough for teaching this class. If it
hadn't been for you I would have given up on scrapbooking.
I had completely lost the desire to continue with a hobby I
at one time had loved. The burden of chronology had stolen
the desire from me.
My LOM system is now in place and I enjoy scrapbooking more
than ever. It is truly about the memories now and not trying to
be caught up. One of my favorite points of the class was the
category drawers and the connections you asked us to find in them.
I love doing layouts from the connections I find.
Thank you for BPS and LOM,
Dawn aka scrapalife
Cherry Valley, Massachusetts

105

Age 29

Biologist

Lives in Whitehorse,
Yukon, Canada

Expecting her first child

Scrapbooker for 4 years

Storage Albums:
3-ring photo albums

Category Drawers:
Nexxt Studio Photo Box
with photo dividers

Library Albums:
12 x 12 3-ring cloth
albums from American
Crafts (black, red, green,
and blue)

Michelle Sicotte

Before Library of Memories

Michelle had always stored her photos in albums
in date order—but that was the extent of her
organizational system. She had no interest in
scrapbooking chronologically, but since she was
organized that way, she had a tough time breaking
out of the chronological box to tell the stories that
were most meaningful to her. "When I had spare
time to scrapbook," she says, "I didn't feel inspired.
Instead of changing the way I was organized, I would
buy more supplies and spend more time online,
searching for ideas."

As she adapted the Library of Memories to fit her
needs, Michelle fashioned a customized system that
allows her to scrapbook what matters most to her—
without the frustration of wondering where to start.
As she sorted through all her photos, placing pictures
into Storage Binders and Category Drawers, Michelle
was able to review the most meaningful aspects of her
life and gain a new perspective on her hobby.

Her version of Library of Memories

- She personalized her Library Albums, changing
  the titles to: A Life Rich in Love (People We Love),
  Journey Together (Places We Go), Joy for Living
  (Things We Do), and Together Always (All About Us).

- She uses a 5 x 7 two-up photo album for her Photos
  I Love album, placing enlargements in the top
  pocket of each page and journaling in the bottom.

- Because she has only partly converted to digital photography, Michelle keeps things extra simple by sorting her digital photos by month and year.

Case Study: Fetch layout

As Michelle started sorting photos of her dog, Padfoot, she got a good laugh over the many photos she had of him carrying a stick. Seeing the repetitive theme of his obsession with playing fetch, she knew she needed to create a page about it. She and her husband both love the layout because it really offers insight into the personality of the dog they love.

"Now I feel like my scrapbooks are more authentic and better represent my life. Plus, the time I do spend scrapbooking is more productive so I can spend more time enjoying other aspects of my life. And of course, I'm keeping my sweet husband happier with a cleaner, more organized workspace—that is big!"

Age 36

Stay-at-home, home-
schooling mom of three

Lives in Hollister, California

Scrapbooker for 11 years

Storage Albums:
Pioneer 4 x 6 pocket
albums

Category Drawers:
File box from Staples

Library Albums:
8½ x 11 D-ring modern
albums from American
Crafts (red, green, navy,
and brown)

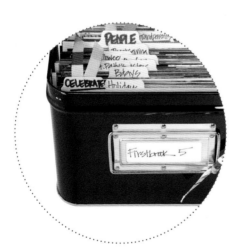

Karen Firstbrook

Before Library of Memories

After storing and scrapbooking her photos chronologically for 10 years, Karen completely changed her approach to her hobby when she adopted the Library of Memories system. Yes, switching from chronological storage to category storage was a huge stretch for her. (She admits there were times when she had to take a deep breath and re-read the Scrapstrong Pledge.)

In all the time she spent digging through mounds of photos, ordering prints from her digital files, and sorting them into meaningful categories, Karen began to look at her scrapbooking desires differently. "It became clear that this chronological system wasn't really working if my end goal had changed from being caught up to creating meaningful scrapbooks for my family," she says. "Chronological scrapping kept my focus on time, places, and people, and it did not create a scrapping atmosphere that focused on meaningful and purposeful journaling."

Her version of Library of Memories

- When she first created her Category Drawers, Karen ran out to Staples and purchased a cute black box and some blank tab cards (instead of buying actual drawers). To begin, she borrowed the categories I have in my drawers, but after her initial triage, it became obvious which categories weren't necessary and which ones she needed to add to my list.

- Looking through the pictures filed in her Things category drawer, Karen realized that her family revels in celebrations, holidays, and traditions. So she renamed her Things We Do category to Days We Celebrate. (See title page, below.)

Case Study: Grandpa's album

With the new focus Karen gained through the Library of Memories system, she was able to easily pay tribute to a departed loved one. After hearing about the passing of her 89-year-old grandpa, she was *immediately* able to find pictures of him in her People We Love drawer and create a quick album for the funeral.

"If Grandpa had passed away before I switched to the Library of Memories system, I would have had to dig through boxes and boxes of chronologically sorted pictures, hoping I could find all of the pictures I've taken of him through the years. When I set up my new organizational system, I had no idea it would one day serve me as we started the grieving process—but it did."

Age 41

Stay-at-home mom
of three

Lives in Dedham,
Massachusetts

Scrapbooker for 10 years

Storage Binders:
3-ring Pioneer albums

Category Drawers:
Power sort box from
Creative Memories

Library Albums:
12 x 12 and 8½ x 11
3-ring linen albums from
Stampin' Up! (red, moss,
navy, and natural)

Maureen Sargent

Before Library of Memories

A longtime scrapbooker, Maureen felt like she was
pretty organized even before she discovered the
Library of Memories system. All of her pictures
were in order, her prints were stored (with
duplicates) in 3-up albums, she had negatives in
sleeves inside a 3-ring binder, and she had several
years of scanned images saved on her computer.
"I had a system—a very detailed one, I might
add—but it didn't support my desire to tell the
important stories. I was so frustrated trying to get
a system set up that worked for me."

By implementing her own approach to the Library
of Memories system, Maureen shifted gears from
chronology to inspiration. Now, thanks to her
new focus, she enjoys scrapbooking individual
memories (like her daughter's cute dress-up
adventures) instead of trying to tackle an entire
year at once.

Her version of Library of Memories
The Life Cycle of a Sargent Photo

1. Take lots of pictures
2. Upload images to Photoshop Elements
3. Review and delete
4. Tag*
5. Fix (red eye, occasional crop)
6. Upload to Snapfish
7. Put best photos in shopping cart*
8. Print monthly*

9. Date stamp back of prints with StazOn* ink

10. Store in 3-up photo albums (Storage Binders)*

11. Scrap what and when I feel like it. When a Storage Binder is all scrapped out:

  11a. Create a year-in-review spread*

  11b. Sort the rest of the photos into Category Drawers*

  11c. Free up the book for a new year*

*New steps since Library of Memories

Case Study: Photos of Colin

Desiring to create a title page for her son's album ("All About Colin"), Maureen was easily able to gather eight photos of him by simply thumbing through the Colin section of her All About Us category drawer. "I just love how this simple little collage represents so much of him over a 10-year span—from his toddler personality, his love of museums, reading, comics and sports, and his fabulous red hair," she says. "I never would have created this snapshot of him before Library of Memories, and if I had tried it would have taken hours and hours, not minutes."

Case Study: Photos I Love

Maureen put her Photos I Love pictures in 8 x 8 page protectors, joined them with a jump ring, and hung them on her scrapbook cabinet with a hook. She hasn't started scrapbooking them yet, but when she does they'll be easily accessible!

3
your
results

Age 36

Executive coach

Lives in Melville, Australia

Expecting her first child

Scrapbooker for 6 years

Storage Binders:
Binders from Albox
Australia

Category Drawers:
Second-hand metal
drawers (purchased online
and spray painted white)

Library Albums:
12 x 12 Urban Chic albums
from All My Memories
(green, pink, blue, and red)

Narelle Jurss

Before Library of Memories

Like many scrapbookers, Narelle was tied to the chronology of her memories. She was afraid to scrapbook out of order or throw out any not-so-fabulous photos, so she was in a constant state of guilt, stress, and creative block. As she proceeded chronologically through her memories, quite often the next photos in line turned out to be mediocre or uninspiring. What could Narelle do but avoid scrapbooking altogether and (get this) clean her house instead? (Now *that's* scary!)

But thanks to her new system, the guilt is long gone. Scrapbooking is a relaxed, enjoyable experience for Narelle now—not a challenge to see how many pages she can churn out. "If I only do two pages this year and they mean something or record something personal or important to me or my family, rather than the obligatory Christmas pages, that's fantastic!"

TITLE PAGE

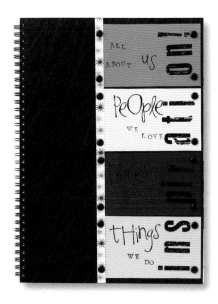

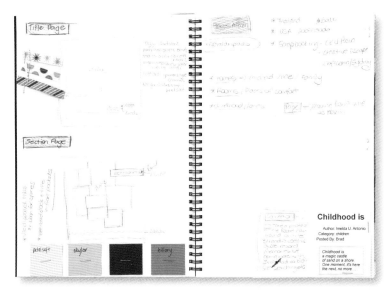

Her version of Library of Memories

- Narelle has an inspiration notebook where she records page ideas and inspiration that may be useful in the future. Before creating her title and section pages for her Library Albums, she sketched out design ideas in her notebook.

- She keeps scrapbook-worthy memorabilia in suspended file folders inside four plastic filing boxes—organized by year or type of memorabilia. She also has an index to help her easily track down specific items when it's their turn to join a layout.

- Narelle is planning to add event-based albums to her Library Albums (one for Christmas, one for weddings, one for birthdays, and so on).

"My new scrapbooking motto is: 'There is no such thing as behind—just lots of fabulous creative adventures ahead.' And it's okay that my Library of Memories system is not finished (not even close). It is a work in progress and that's how I like it; I can change it and refresh it when I feel like it."

Age 38

High school guidance
counselor

Lives in North Easton,
Massachusetts

Mother of three

Scrapbooker for 7 years

Storage Binders:
Pioneer 3-up albums

Category Drawers:
Power Sort Box from
Creative Memories

Library Albums:
12 x 12 Modern albums
from American Crafts
(pink and red)

Joanne Teliszewski

Before Library of Memories

Like many women when they first start scrapbooking, Joanne jumped in with both feet and fell in love with her new hobby. She relished her scrapbooking time and made lots of layouts in the process. But as her family grew, the hectic lifestyle of raising three children drained her creative energy and dampened her commitment to memory keeping.

Learning about the Library of Memories system was the jumpstart Joanne needed to rediscover the joy she once felt in preserving her family's treasured memories. She says when she realized the system had been created by a mother of five who owns her own business, she decided it must be possible for her to add scrapbooking back into her life in a balanced way. And she's right!

Joanne especially loves her Category Drawers because she (finally) has a centralized place to store photos. No more hunting through boxes and envelopes! "More importantly, I have no excuse not to pull out some photos and do a scrapbook page during naptime or when I have a few hours on a weekend night," she says.

Her version of Library of Memories

- To save money, Joanne bought a Power Sort Box from Creative Memories instead of investing in metal Category Drawers. Since she often scrapbooks away from home, the portability of her Category Box better suits the way she works.

I can never remember whether it snowed for six days and six nights when I was twelve or whether it snowed twelve days and twelve nights when I was six.
~Dylan Thomas

TITLE PAGE FOR "ALL ABOUT US" ALBUM

- Instead of buying 8½ x 11 Library Albums *and* 12 x 12 Library Albums, she made her 12 x 12 albums work for both layout sizes— using a combination of both sizes of page protectors inside.

- Rather than worrying about whether her title and section pages match the exterior of her albums, Joanne has decided to choose colors as she goes. This flexibility will help her enjoy each project instead of wasting energy worrying about whether everything matches.

Case Study: Popsicle Page

As she sorted through her photos, Joanne discovered three great pictures, taken over the span of three summers, of her young son enjoying a Popsicle. She immediately knew she needed to create a layout featuring all three photos that shows off the connection she discovered. (And you can bet she'll continue taking pictures of him

with his much-loved Popsicles, now that she has sees them as a recurring favorite.)

"I no longer feel overwhelmed and behind. Instead, I'm focusing on the memories that I want to record and that I hope my children and future generations will appreciate," she says.

Age 43

Photographer and
substitute elementary
school teacher

Lives in Moss Vale, New
South Wales, Australia

Mother of six

Scrapbooker for 5 years

Storage Binders:
Pioneer 3-ring albums

Category Drawers:
Photo box

Library Albums:
12 x 12 D-ring cloth binders
from American Crafts (blue,
green, pink, and brown)

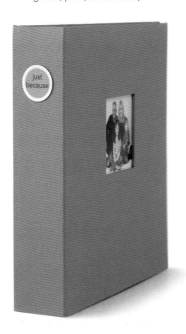

Rachelle Harvey

Before Library of Memories

Rachelle says the Library of Memories system
was her last-ditch effort to find an efficient
and liberating approach that would allow her
to enjoy her hobby again. And thankfully, what
she discovered has totally changed the way she
scrapbooks. "I now have more freedom than
ever before and here is the kicker, I also have
more control. I can scrap when I am inspired
because I know I can find the perfect photo in
my Category File."

Her version of Library of Memories

In addition to her four Library Albums, Rachelle
also needed a Birthdays album to house the eight
inevitable birthday layouts she creates for her
family members each year. Having this album in
her collection satisfies her need for chronological
scrapbooking, and it's a fun collection of her
family's favorite celebrations.

She also added an 8½ x 11 album (the same brand
and color as her All About Us album) to her Library
Albums, titling it "Just Because." This smaller
album is the place where she stores inspiration-
based layouts that don't necessarily have a strong
tie to one of the four main albums in her collection.

Catherine Allan

Before Library of Memories

Catherine discovered the Library of Memories system during a time of transition in her family. With kids leaving home, getting married, and having children of their own, she was ready to forget about "catching up."

"I honestly don't know how I functioned without this philosophy in the past," she says. "The scrapping I did before seems so connected to dates and events. Not that it's a bad thing, but I find myself now connecting memories in such different ways."

Her version of Library of Memories

For the most part, Catherine followed my system as I've outlined it in chapters 1 and 2, but she did make a few changes to fit her life. For example, she doesn't do the School of Life albums because four of her children are already out of public school, and she feels no need to work backwards.

Case Study: Uncanny Resemblance

While sorting photos, Catherine stumbled upon a school picture of herself and some school pictures of her children. She always thought she and her oldest son looked alike, but seeing these photos together confirmed it. She never would have made this connection or this layout without following the Library of Memories approach to sorting and organizing photos.

Age 48

Homemaker and former nurse

Lives in Twin Falls, Idaho

Mother of six and grandmother of one

Scrapbooker for 11 years

Storage Binders:
Pioneer 3-ring albums

Category Drawers:
4 x 6 filing drawers from Office Depot

Library Albums:
8½ x 11 albums from American Crafts (brown, red, green, and blue)

3 *your* results

Age 61

Travel agent

Lives in Half Moon Bay,
California

Mother of two and
grandmother of two

Scrapbooker for 9 years

Storage Binders:
3-up albums from Target

Category Drawers:
2-drawer units from
Croppin' Companion

Library Albums:
12 x 12 Modern albums
from American Crafts (blue,
pink, brown and green)

Donna Bettencourt

Before Library of Memories

A perpetual organizer, Donna thought she had her scrapbooking stuff under control. But, after learning about Library of Memories, she tweaked her setup so she has more creative freedom (and still knows where everything is). "It's a great feeling to have a place for everything and everything in its place," she says.

How Things Have Changed

Getting rid of not-so-great photos was a huge breakthrough for Donna—something that has really changed the way she views her pictures. "I can toss bad photos without guilt because I realized they're only paper; they're not my actual children!"

Donna's approach to journaling has also evolved since she created her own Library of Memories. Since she is more in touch with the emotions attached to her photos, she journals from her own perspective more frequently. And she's no longer afraid to scrapbook about herself, because she realizes that one purpose of her hobby is to reveal the real Donna. (You go, girl!)

Favorite Things

Donna especially loves her Library Albums, so much so that she's prepared a few extra albums to house the many layouts she knows she'll be making. "I have four Library albums all done and covered, complete with labels and title pages—plus two extra albums that are covered and ready to go for future expansion," she says. "It was so easy to file some layouts recently and slip them right where they belonged."

Laurie Rhodes

Age 50

Bank customer service

Lives in Tega Cay, South Carolina

Mother of two

Scrapbooker for 10 years

Storage Binders:
Blue 3-up albums from
Me & My Big Ideas

Category Drawers:
Photo boxes

Library Albums:
12 x 12 linen albums from
We R Memory Keepers
(orange zest, wedgewood,
avocado, and eggplant)

Before Library of Memories

Laurie was a devoted chronological scrapbooker until 2003, when her mother passed away. She realized she hadn't taken many pictures (especially of her mother) that year, and she didn't have the enthusiasm to do much scrapbooking. In the years that followed, she did some event-based scrapbooking here and there, but because she was so tied to chronology, she didn't know where to store her layouts or what to do about the missing years.

How Things Have Changed

Now, with the help of a personalized Library of Memories system, Laurie feels free to scrapbook the memories that inspire her, in any order she chooses. "Separating my pages into People We Love, Places We Go, Things We Do, and All About Us was a freeing experience," she says. "I'm now able to keep current *and* tackle my older pictures. And every completed layout will have a home."

Favorite Things

Laurie's favorite activity was the Start Here jar (see page 78). Whenever she has free time, she pulls out a stick and completes the activity written there. She modified her container by adding a Start Again spot where she places the sticks after working on the task for the time she has available. "This way I know I have worked on each step once and I'm ready to start again. Library of Memories is a process, and I'm always ready to start again and not feel guilty that I'm never finished," she says.

Age 40

Stay-at-home mom

Lives in Trabuco Canyon,
California

Mother of four

Scrapbooker for 9 years

Storage Binders:
Pioneer 3-up albums

Category Drawers:
5 x 7 drawers from Staples

Library Albums:
12 x 12 Modern albums
from American Crafts
(green, red, blue, and
brown)

TITLE PAGE

Tamara Morrison

Before Library of Memories

Before discovering Library of Memories, Tamara stored her digital photos chronologically on her computer—but she also had 20 years' worth of prints shoved in various boxes and drawers. "I needed to revamp my organizational approach to reflect the way I wanted to scrapbook," she says.

Although Tamara generally doesn't scrapbook her memories chronologically, her photos were organized in date order, rather than reflecting her inspiration-based approach to the hobby. "When I had an idea, I would get frustrated sifting through folders of digital images or dusty boxes trying to find just the right photos," she says.

Her version of Library of Memories

Now, with her new system in place, she can act on creative inspiration quickly because her photos are easy to find, and they're organized according to the themes she generally scrapbooks about. "Fine-tuning my approach to scrapbooking also fine-tuned my approach to photography and my appreciation for the seemingly mundane little details that define my family. The way I live and the way I record my life are in sync now, and both are better because of it," she says.

Tamara changed the title of her Things We Do album to Things That Matter in order to better encompass the non-verb things—like seasons, colors, technology, and sentimental belongings—that matter to her family.

Kathryn Benfiet

Age 48

Marketing event
coordinator

Lives in Portland, Oregon

Mother of one

Scrapbooker for 15 years

Storage Binders:
Hanging file folders and
filing cabinet

Category Drawers:
5 x 8 lidded boxes from
Office Depot

Library Albums:
3-ring Pioneer 12 x 12
binders (black)

Before Library of Memories

After scrapbooking chronologically for years,
Kathryn experienced a wake-up call when she was
diagnosed with a potentially fatal liver disease
in 2003. With a full year of chemotherapy ahead
of her, she wanted to fast-track her scrapbooking
and get a few albums done for her daughter and
husband. She knew her chronological approach
wouldn't work anymore, so she switched gears to a
more memory-based approach to her hobby.

How Things Have Changed

With cancer treatments in the past, Kathryn has
continued with her non-chronological methods.
As she adapted the Library of Memories system
to meet her needs, she made even more changes
in her life that have enhanced her creative hobby.
"My new system is a way of life, an attitude," she
says. "It helps me to be more in the moment and
always aware of the memories we're making."

She says it has also changed the way she takes
photos. While sorting her pictures into Category
Drawers, Kathryn discovered that she hadn't
taken photos of the things that really tell her
family's story. Now she is much more aware of the
meaningful details she wants to remember, and
she spends time capturing those with her camera
instead of taking generic event shots.

Age 44

Certified public accountant

Lives in Glenhaven, Australia

Mother of two

Scrapbooker for 4 years

Storage Binders:
Cardboard photo boxes

Category Drawers:
Cardboard photo boxes

Library Albums:
12 x 12 D-ring binders from
Love You More (pink, blue,
purple, red, and green)

Julia Colli

Case Study: Tent Page

Since discovering the Library of Memories approach to scrapbooking, Julia has become much more aware of moments, focusing less on events. She was inspired to take the photo on the layout below after realizing that the laundry she'd just hung out to dry closely resembled the tents her children used to make with blankets when they were young. Had she been in the chronology-centered perspective of her pre-Library of Memories days, she may have missed the connection.

Her version of Library of Memories

After finishing a layout, Julia displays it on a little easel for everyone to enjoy—until she completes her next layout. Then she moves it into a special album (a happy green one!), where all of her recently completed layouts live for a while. Every six months or so, she files them away into their final homes (the appropriate Library Albums). That way if visiting family members want to peek at her latest layouts, they're all in one place.

Brooke Schumacher

Before Library of Memories

When she first heard about the Library of Memories system, Brooke absolutely loved the liberating notion of scrapping "out of order" (as she puts it). But she had no idea there was a whole photo-organizing system to support it.

"Now all of my photos, even digital ones, are in storage albums that all of us can look through, and all of my digital photo files are organized by year," she says. "I can find photos when I am looking for them. I have permission to scrap the photos that are most meaningful to me, not the ones that come next, so I enjoy scrapping much more. As a result, I feel less guilt about my scrapbooking, and I am much more creative."

Favorite Things

When beginning a theme album or a series of pages that will use similar papers and supplies, Brooke assembles a Materials File. She uses oversize plastic page pouches to hold the elements of her soon-to-be created projects. She stores her Materials Files vertically on a bookshelf, each labeled with a metal-rimmed tag. "My Materials Files really help me return to a project where I left off. I can perform the creative process of choosing papers and embellishments once. Then, even if I have to put it away and come back to it later, my supplies, ideas, and unfinished work are all in one place," she says.

Age 42

Stay-at-home mom
and former obstetrician/
gynecologist

Lives in Dhahran,
Saudi Arabia

Mother of three

Scrapbooker for 4 years

Storage Binders:
12 x 12 post-bound albums
from Close to My Heart

Category Drawers:
Photo box

Library Albums:
3-ring albums (12 x 12 size)
from Stampin' Up! (natural,
red, moss, and navy blue)

Resources

Timeline Worksheet

A timeline is an indispensable tool for sorting decades of photos (see page 46). Begin your timeline with the year you were born or the year you were married, depending on the photos you're sorting. Start listing major events in column two, such as moves, new jobs, births, big vacations, etc., and include the year in column one. Now go back and list the people you want to track (children or siblings) in the remaining columns. As you move down each person's column, fill in his or her age or school grade for each major event. Make copies of this sheet or create your own.

YEAR OF EVENT	LIST OF MAJOR EVENTS AND HIGHLIGHTS	PERSON'S AGE/GRADE AT TIME OF EVENT		
		NAME:	NAME:	NAME:

chapter 1
RESOURCES

pages 16–17
Pioneer storage binders, *scrapbook.com*

DYMO label maker, *dymo.com*

page 18
Steel Master 2-drawer card cabinet, *staples.com*
note: *I ordered my category drawers at Staples.com. But drawers like these can also be special-ordered from some office-supply stores and catalogs. Or, there's always eBay!*

page 20
D-ring Modern Albums, *americancrafts.com*

page 24
iPhoto from iLife, *apple.com*

page 26
Nesting folders, *croppincompanion.com*

page 28
File tote, *rubbermaid.com*

page 30
Drawers from Memory Dock system, 8¼ x 14, *weronthenet.com*

page 32
Suitcase box, *amazon.com*
note: *I found my cultural memorabilia box at my local TJ Maxx, but you can purchase something similar at Amazon.com. Simply go to the "Beauty" section and search for "suitcase box."*

page 34
Notebooks and wooden recipe box, *target.com*
note: *These items can be purchased almost anywhere. I'm always picking up cute little note pads here and there! Target.com has several varieties of recipe boxes—even wood, like mine. From the homepage, search for "wood recipe box."*

page 36
Archival shoe boxes for photos, *archivalmethods.com*
note: *Two wonderful resources for archival storage items are archivalmethods.com (search for "archival shoe boxes") and exposuresonline.com (search for "original shoe box storage").*

page 37
Plastic drawers, *sterilite.com*
note: *I picked up my square-punch picture drawers at a discount retailer years ago. However, an online resource I like for Sterilite and Iris brand containers is coastalbaycompany.com (click on "Storage Drawers" from the homepage).*

chapter 2
RESOURCES

page 43
celebrate who you are
materials mini album • **note** this was a gift from Tia Bennett

page 53
happy childhood album
materials 9 x 9 leather album (Making Memories) • patterned paper • clear flowers (Heidi Swapp) • brads (Queen & Co.) • ric rac • photo corners (salvaged from old baby book)

page 57
love
materials patterned papers (American Crafts, Daisy D's) • leather flower, brad (Making Memories) • 12 x 12 page

page 73
cutting mat and craft knife (Doodlebug Design)

page 77
things we do library album
and framework pages
materials Modern Album (American Crafts) • large foam letter stamps (Making Memories) • metal rimmed circle tags (Avery) • small alphabet stamps (Hero Arts) • stamping ink (Stampin' Up!) • ribbon (Offray) • 8½ x 11 album and pages • **note** these small, colorful bull-dog clips came from the dollar section of Target

page 78
idea journal
materials metal and felt letters (American Crafts) • chipboard letters (Pressed Petals, Making Memories)

page 79
start here jar
materials jar • patterned paper (Daisy D's) • rub on letters (American Crafts) • gingham ribbon (Offray)

page 81
grandma addie
materials patterned paper (Scenic Route Paper Co.) • ghost flower, page tab (Heidi Swapp) • brad (Making Memories) • journaling card (7gypsies) • 8½ x 11 page

page 82
tooth fairy tales
materials patterned papers (My Mind's Eye, Scenic Route Paper Co.) • transparent screen print (Hambly Studios) • stickers (Karen Foster Design) • vellum envelope (EK Success) • jewels (Heidi Swapp) • tab punch (McGill) • Signo Impact white pen (Uni-ball) • Century Gothic font • 12 x 12 page

page 83

we swim

materials patterned papers (Doodlebug Design, Provo Craft) • chipboard letters (American Crafts) • ribbon (KI Memories, Offray) • date stamp (Stampin' Up!) • fabric tab (Scrapworks) • beaded chain • 8½ x 11 spread

page 85

birthday boy

materials patterned paper, sticker (Pebbles Inc.) • chipboard number (Maya Road) • transparent overlay (My Mind's Eye) • ric rac • staples • Century Gothic font • 11 x 8½ spread

page 86

clark's friends

materials chipboard letters (Pressed Petals, Chatterbox, KI Memories, Heidi Swapp) • dimensional letter stickers (American Crafts) • ribbon (Strano Designs) • epoxy stickers (Love, Elsie) • 12 x 12 spread

page 87

create t-shirt

materials patterned papers (My Mind's Eye, Hambly Studios, Adornit) • transparency (Hambly Studios) • journaling notes, chipboard flower (Heidi Swapp) • ribbon, ric rac (Adornit, American Crafts, Maya Road) • 8½ x 11 spread

page 89

oh brother section page

materials alphabet stamps (Hero Arts) • stamping ink (Stampin' Up!) • metal rimmed tag (Avery) • ribbon (Offray) • 8½ x 11 page

pages 90–93

photos i love albums

materials 8 x 8 linen albums (We R Memory Keepers) • Picture It Page Frames acrylic frames (Pageframe Designs)

clark title page

materials chipboard letters (Chatterbox, Maya Road, Making Memories, Pressed Petals) • square punch (Fiskars) • 8 x 8 page

famous last words

materials note paper • alphabet stamps • 8 x 8 page

no title

materials patterned paper, metal rimmed tag (Making Memories) • Carolee's Creations metal star (Adornit) • decorative tape (Heidi Swapp) • 8 x 8 page

life is good

materials patterned papers (Scenic Route Paper Co., Kellie Crowe) • acrylic accent (KI Memories) • button (EK Success) • 8 x 8 page

trey page

materials patterned papers (Collage Press, Bo-Bunny) • chipboard letters (We R Memory Keepers) • metal photo corners (American Crafts) • journaling spots (Heidi Swapp) • epoxy accents (KI Memories) • game piece • staples • 8 x 8 page

taft page

materials patterned paper scraps • felt accent (American Crafts) • acrylic accents (KI Memories) • Carolee's Creations printed ribbon (Adornit) • velvet ribbon (American Crafts) • fabric tag (Scrapworks) • staples • 8 x 8 page

page 92

Quote is from *Everyday Creativity and New Views of Human Nature: Psychological, Social, and Spiritual Perspectives*, edited by Ruth Richards (American Psychological Association, 2007)

page 94–95

hanging tag books

materials chipboard books (Maya Road) • white rub-on letters (American Crafts) • striped patterned papers • acrylic paint

page 96–99

london page

materials paper flowers (Prima) • felt flower (American Crafts) • blue paper tag (Creativity Inc.) • patterned paper • tags • 8½ x 11 spread

london photo album

materials photo album (Umbra) • patterned papers (BasicGrey) • dimensional letters (Li'l Davis Designs) • rub ons (American Crafts) • 2-up photo album

travel inspiration book

materials 5 x 7 chipboard book (Maya Road) • patterned paper (Doodlebug Design) • heart accent (Heidi Swapp) • ribbon

page 100–101

happy colors

materials tag book (C&T Publishing) • ribbon (Strano Designs) • epoxy sticker (Love, Elsie) • patterned paper (Die Cuts With a View, My Mind's Eye, Scenic Route Paper Co., Close To My Heart, Daisy D's, Pebbles Inc.) • various bits and pieces from my stash • **note** cover image is a postcard from *littlemissmatched.com*

chapter 3
RESOURCES

page 106

a life rich in love

materials patterned papers (7gypsies, BasicGrey, Scenic Route Paper Co.) • circle punches (McGill, EK Success) • brads (Making Memories) • dye inkpad (Vivid) • black Pigment Pro Pen (American Crafts) • letter stamps (Hero Arts) • 12 x 12 page by Michelle Sicotte, Whitehorse, YT, Canada

page 107

fetch

materials patterned papers (BasicGrey, Chatterbox) • sticker (Autumn Leaves) • paw embellishments (American Traditional Designs) • 12 x 12 page by Michelle Sicotte

page108

file box (Staples)

in the end...

In essence, *Photo Freedom* is about finding the time and the inspiration to celebrate the people, places, and things you love most in your scrapbooks.

Trust yourself

Believe that you have the answers you're looking for. There's nothing wrong with asking others for advice and sharing ideas of your own, but the success of your customized Library of Memories system ultimately depends on you trusting your intuition.

Trust the system

Remember that as you move photos into and out of your Storage Binders, they'll go through an automatic "priority" filter. If you find you've passed over certain pictures for 3 or 4 years, give yourself permission to let go of them and move on. Save a few for your Category Drawers, place the rest lovingly in Cold Storage, and refill that Storage Binder with newer pictures and fresher memories.

Don't over-plan

We often take or print out pictures because we have specific projects in mind, and this is a good thing. But make sure you're flexible enough with your plans that you allow inspiration to have a role in the process. Who knows? You may be inspired to try something altogether different and more meaningful than your original idea. Also, please don't try and decide right now what and how you will scrapbook in the future. The Library of Memories system is set up to support ongoing inspiration, and as long as you go with the flow, and allow the system to work, your enthusiasm will be sustained.

Have fun!

Scrapbooking is fun. Soak it all up—the colors, the pretty papers, the amazing possibilities. Enjoy the process, and welcome the profound influence this hobby can have on your everyday perspective. Above all, don't forget about the big picture: your scrapbooks are a reflection of your unique life, and you have the chance (and the choice) to live your life fully and happily.

Start now! *Stacy*

You have exactly enough time to scrapbook the memories that are most important to you.

To learn more about Stacy Julian's scrapbooking approach and philosophy, pick up a copy of her book, *The Big Picture: Scrapbook Your Life and a Whole Lot More*, available at your local retailer or through **simplescrapbooksmag.com**. For personal coaching (and cheerleading!) from Stacy as you create your own personal Library of Memories, take her online class at **bigpicturescrapbooking.com**.

Simple
Scrapbooks™